3702697322

D1333339

WOMEN IN SOCIETY
A Feminist List edited by
Jo Campling

Editorial Advisory Group

The last two decades have seen an explosion of publishing by,
about and for women. This list is designed to make a particular
contribution to this continuing process by commissioning and
publishing books which consolidate and advance feminist research
and debate in key areas in a form suitable for students, academics
and researchers but also accessible to a broader general readership.

As far as possible, the books adopt an international perspective,
incorporating comparative material from a range of countries
where this is illuminating. Above all, they are interdisciplinary,
aiming to put women's studies and feminist discussion firmly on
the agenda in subject areas as disparate as law, literature, art and
social policy.

WOMEN IN SOCIETY
A Feminist List edited by
Jo Campling

Published

Christy Adair **Women and Dance: sylphs and sirens**
Sheila Allen and Carol Wolkowitz **Homeworking: myths and realities**
Ros Ballaster, Margaret Beetham, Elizabeth Frazer and Sandrda Hebron **Women's Worlds: ideology, femininity and the woman's magazine**
Jenny Beale **Women in Ireland: voices of change**
Jennifer Breen **In Her Own Write: twentieth-century women's fiction**
Valerie Bryson **Feminist Political Theory: an introduction**
Ruth Carter and Gill Kirkup **Women in Engineering: a good place to be?**
Joan Chandler **Women without Husbands: an exploration of the margins of marriage**
Gillian Dalley **Ideologies of Caring: rethinking community and collectivism** (2nd edn)
Emily Driver and Audrey Droisen (*editors*) **Child Sexual Abuse: feminist perspectives**
Elizabeth Ettorre **Women and Substance Use**
Elizabeth Fallaize **French Women's Writing: recent fiction**
Lesley Ferris **Acting Women: images of women in theatre**
Diana Gittins **The Family in Question: changing households and familiar ideologies** (2nd edn)
Tuula Gordon **Feminist Mothers**
Tuula Gordon **Single Women: on the margins?**
Frances Gray **Women and Laughter**
Eileen Green, Diana Woodward and Sandra Hebron **Women's Leisure, What Leisure?**
Frances Heidensohn **Women and Crime** (2nd edn)
Ursula King **Women and Spirituality: voices of protest and promise** (2nd edn)
Jo Little, Linda Peake and Pat Richardson (*editors*) **Women in Cities: gender and the urban environment**
Susan Lonsdale **Women and Disability: the experience of physical disability among women**
Mavis Maclean **Surviving Divorce: women's resources after separation**
Shelley Pennington and Belinda Westover **A Hidden Workforce: homeworkers in England, 1850–1985**
Vicky Randall **Women and Politics: an international perspective** (2nd edn)
Diane Richardson **Women, Motherhood and Childrearing**
Susan Sellers **Language and Sexual Difference: feminist writing in France**
Patricia Spallone **Beyond Conception: the new politics of reproduction**
Taking Liberties Collective **Learning the Hard Way: women's oppression and men's education**
Clare Ungerson (*editor*) **Women and Social Policy: a reader**
Kitty Warnock **Land Before Honour: Palestinian women in the Occupied Territories**
Annie Woodhouse **Fantastic Women: sex, gender and transvestism**

Ideologies of Caring

Rethinking Community and Collectivism

Second Edition

Gillian Dalley

Foreword by Margot Jefferys

MACMILLAN

in association with the Centre for Policy on Ageing

First edition 1988
Reprinted three times
Second edition 1996

Published by
MACMILLAN PRESS LTD
Houndmills, Basingstoke, Hampshire RG21 2XS
and London
Companies and representatives
throughout the world

ISBN 0–333–65097–2 hardcover
ISBN 0–333–65098–0 paperback

A catalogue record for this book is available
from the British Library.

10 9   8   7   6   5   4   3   2   1
05 04 03 02 01 00 99 98 97 96

Editing and origination by
Aardvark Editorial, Suffolk

Printed in Malaysia

For Jessie and to the memory of Jack

Contents

Foreword

I must start with a confession. When I was asked to write a foreword to this second revised edition of *Ideologies of Caring*, I had not read the first which appeared in 1988. My initial reaction to the invitation was one of some reluctance. I had already a long list of books and articles which I intended to read and review. Nevertheless, because I had had the opportunity recently to admire the author's calm competence as Director of the Centre for Policy on Ageing, I decided that I wanted to know whether her contribution to the literature relating to some of the most salient issues facing modern society – how to provide care to all those with dependency needs without exploiting the carers – was as great as her obvious capacity to give leadership to one of the major 'think tanks' in the field of social policy.

I am now grateful to the editor of the series and the publishers for pressing me to read the manuscript, and feel honoured by their invitation to make this contribution. The book itself needs no foreword from me. Its introduction sets the scene admirably. It notes in passing the way in which acceptable language relating to disability has changed in less than a decade in response to the increasing role played by disabled people themselves in controlling their own destinies. It records the events and trends of the last few years which have underlined the cogency of the case for examining thoughtfully and thoroughly the tensions and contradictions surrounding the way in which modern societies define dependency, seek to provide for those deemed to be dependant, and assign the task of caring to paid and unpaid agents.

The substantive chapters themselves utilize concepts drawn from social and political philosophy, dwelling particularly on those of freedom and altruism, individualism and collectivism. These are used to analyse historical developments and contemporary approaches to caring as a societal as well as a familial responsibility. Interwoven throughout is the contribution to our understanding which has come from an appreciation of the continued gendered aspect of caring functions, illuminated by the work of feminist theoreticians. No facile solutions are offered. Indeed, the impartial student of social policy and caring professional worker will find food for thoughtful reconsideration of much of the received wisdom of the early welfare state years rather than the reiteration of tired dogmas from the political left or right or other entrenched religious or ideological positions.

MARGOT JEFFERYS
Emeritus Professor of Medical Sociology
University of London

Acknowledgements

The origins of this book lie mainly in the early 1980s when my research interests in community care began to develop, but in one sense they go further back than that to the days, more than twenty years ago, when I was directly involved in the women's movement. It is from that time that the significance of the collectivist principle, as a means of addressing some of the wrongs that women experienced, derives. More recently, as the policy of community care has become a live political and social issue, my interests – partly because of career changes along the way – have become more practically focused, involved as much with the concerns of policy implementation as with conceptual issues. When I wrote the first edition of this book, community care was not seen as the major health and social care issue that it is today. Relatively little was written about it. The past decade has seen a mushrooming of interest in the subject within the academic, policy and practice worlds alike. However, I still believe that the issues that I raised then are salient today. I may have modified some of my views in the light of further debate, but the core propositions remain the same: that our current way of viewing the solutions to dependency and caring are fastbound in ideological preconceptions about the primacy of the family above all other social forms and that adopting a collectivist approach to the issues might prove more rewarding.

My thanks are due to all the friends and colleagues who have stimulated my thinking over the years – either through outright disagreement, or through guarded or sometimes forthright support. The first time round, I thanked my three children for ensuring that I kept a sense of proportion about the business of writing. They still do even though they are now grown up – and, again, I thank them. And, of course, thanks go to Jo Campling for encouraging me to take another look at this book and appreciation to her for the contribution that her editorship of this series has made to social policy studies in general.

GILLIAN DALLEY

Introduction

I wrote the original edition of this book in 1987, and in many ways it feels like an age ago. I said then that the process of writing a book is an enterprise of exploration and that the finished product unexpectedly turns out to be very different from the one originally anticipated. I find now that the process of *revisiting* a book has some of the same impact of surprise. This may partly be due to changes that I have undergone in terms of my own thinking, but more importantly I think that it is because of the dramatic changes in the spirit of the times.

I started out by being interested in questions that arose from the relationship between feminism, notions of collectivism and the policies that present-day social and political institutions have laid down for the care of 'chronically sick and dependent' people (known broadly as community care policies). Like many women of my generation, I had been involved in the women's movement during the 1970s and supported the demands that the movement made for a reappraisal of the structures of daily living. This involved, in particular, a call for greater emphasis to be placed on the communal sharing of domestic tasks – especially in relation to the tasks of caring – and for an end to the gendered division of labour in both the private and public domains. These demands were clearly linked with the collectivist aims to which earlier social and political movements had also subscribed, but in stressing the political nature of the personal (or private) domain, the women's movement took them a stage further.

Since the beginning, however, feminists have been only too aware of the strength of the ideological and structural forces that operate against their attempts to change the world. This is nowhere demonstrated more clearly than in relation to the underlying principles of current community care policies. These appear to be precisely those principles to which feminists are opposed – that is, those relating to the primacy of the family and the home-defined status of women within it. They are exact contradictions of the collectivist solutions to the problems of caring that feminists might propose.

While recognizing the strength of the structural and ideological barriers, I became interested in examining the reasons why this should be so. My research interests up until then had focused on the attitudes of health and social work professionals about where the balance of responsibility for caring lay between family and state. While many believed strongly that the state had an overriding, collective duty to provide care, a significant proportion believed very firmly in the importance of family responsibility and the paramount necessity of maintaining people at home. It occurred to me that many of these individuals might regard themselves as feminists, or at least as advocates of the feminist viewpoint. How great, in that case, must the persuasive strength of familist ideology be for them to give it such unquestioned support.

It was for this reason that I wanted to look more closely at what this signified, to examine some of the component parts of this formidable structure and to look for alternatives – by looking for evidence from past times and from other places to see whether the possessive individualism that seemed to lie at the heart of familist ideology was and has been everywhere uncontested.

This, then, was how it started. Returning to the book almost ten years later, I am conscious of how much has changed in the social and political circumstances that surround us. Women's participation in the labour force has changed and continues to increase substantially, sections of the male population have suffered more extremely than women in relation to unemployment throughout the recession of the late 1980s and beyond, and patterns of childbearing suggest a shift in many women's attitudes to their potential role as mothers. Furthermore, demographic changes are working through, and the increase in the numbers of older people in the population, much talked about in the 1970s and early 1980s, has arrived. The scale of informal caring has mushroomed and, along with the future of long-term care, is a live political issue in a way that it was not ten years ago. It has moved out of the research arena and into the light of public debate. Residential care has been a growth industry, with the development of independent sector care homes, sheltered housing and retirement apartments. In addition, the way in which the development of community care now absorbs much of the total activity of social services departments in a way unthinkable in the past demonstrates its significance in general policy terms.

Although some might suggest that, in some senses, all this undermines the case that I was making nearly ten years ago, I would, however, argue that many of the underlying issues that I was originally concerned with remain the same. Much of the debate about caring and the provision of care is still premised on the principle of familist ideology; much of it fails to examine the case that there is to be made for a collectivist approach to caring and an extension of state responsibility rather than a retrenchment (as is currently happening in the NHS).

The structure of this revised edition therefore remains much as it was and follows the same sequence as before. At the same time, however, I have tried to take into account some of the developments that have taken place during the past decade. One further point needs to be considered – the question of terminology. Ten years ago, it was accept-able to use the terms 'mental handicap', 'dependent', 'elderly', 'mentally ill' and 'disabled'. These terms have subsequently been called into question by both those working in the field or those who themselves fall within those designations. At the same time, at a more general level, the tendency to redefine commonly used terminology in an attempt to change the reality that they represent has been widespread.

My view is that reality cannot be redefined by the good intentions of the few and that, in trying to do so, we end up with a constrained and restricted language that is itself impaired to no good effect (Dalley, 1991). Furthermore, people who may have valuable contri-butions to make are implicitly judged and penalized by their failure to use newly appropriate terminology and thus excluded from the narrow community of the self-righteously correct. In some cases, the decision to adopt particular terminology may have a precise and valid rationale – for example, in the case of physically impaired people choosing to call themselves disabled, meaning that they are disabled by the constraints that society places on them. Nevertheless, the general tendency to move terminology on is not so rationally and analytically based: it is too often the outcome of wishful supposition. In revisiting this book, I have had to make difficult decisions about whether or not to modify the terminology that I have used. I accept to a large degree the argument about the use of the term 'disabled' and have tended to adopt it throughout, although not exclusively. I have tended to avoid the use of the term 'mental handicap' and some of the other examples mentioned above, but I have to admit that my decision to do so is largely governed by my lack of willingness to remain outside the conventions of the day and not necessarily from any conviction that it is correct.

The first chapter is concerned with setting out some of the issues descriptively, in particular the development of community care policies and what they mean for women and for dependent people. Furthermore, it explores the meaning of caring, especially in relation to the differential effects it has for women on the one hand and men on the other. The second chapter takes up these issues and relates them to an analysis of familism, which, it is suggested, structures the whole social organization of daily living and thus directly produces the forms of caring that cause such difficulty for partners in a caring relationship. I am also concerned in this second chapter with linking the analysis of familism to the wider ideology of possessive individualism, which, it has been argued, has underpinned so many social forms – especially family forms – since at least as far back in Britain as the Middle Ages. So far then, this provides a descriptive analysis of how and why things are the way they are.

In the third chapter, I begin to consider alternatives. It is argued that there are other competing ideological forces that social and political movements through the ages have championed, collectivism being one of them. The thinking of the feminist movement over the past century, in relation to collectivism, is used as an example. I examine the notion of collectivism, identifying its component parts and contrasting them with current notions of community. It is suggested that collectivism can relate to both the private and the public domain, to both the social organization of daily living and the social organization of wider society. It is both a structural principle and a moral concept.

Chapter 4 is concerned with the idea of collectivism from a wider perspective, taking, especially, ethnographic and historical examples of the collectivist approach to the organization of daily living and examining how far such examples have or have not proved beneficial for women. I have tried to construct a typology of forms that can be defined according to historical tradition, 'strength' of patriarchy and the degree of solidarity fostered amongst women. Another aspect of collectivism is discussed in the fifth chapter, again using ethnographic and historical evidence. Here there is less concern with the social organization of daily living and more with the moral concept of 'responsibility' as it relates to the fundamental goals of collectivism, notably in respect of the provision of support and care for the dependent.

In Chapter 6 I move from the past (and the present) and from what was (or is) to a concern with models of collective living that might properly be applied to contemporary conditions in the future. Questions are asked concerning the guiding criteria upon which any attempt to develop such forms should be based and whether there is evidence from various parts of the world to suggest they might be feasible.

Finally the last chapter attempts to link rather disparate themes – the issue of caring, feminist critiques of contemporary social policies, the historical tradition of collectivism in its various aspects and feasible models for future collectivist provision of care – and set them against the contemporary political scene. Recent political history saw a move to the right in many Western countries, but that move in itself prompted under pressure, in Britain at least, a response from the left, which began to challenge much of the received wisdom of the 'traditional' left; it began to recognize the need to rethink many of its past assumptions. Now, in the mid-1990s, the supremacy of the right is at last beginning to be seriously challenged. The task now is to ensure that some of the policies and attitudes that characterized the right while it was in the ascendant and which the centre and the left had begun to accept as the norm are rigorously questioned and overturned. I would argue that feminist thinking can play a significant part in this process. This book attempts to do just that.

1

Community care and the meaning of caring

This is a book about dependent people and women who usually care for them. Further than that, it is about ideology – the pattern of beliefs and attitudes that underlie action. In particular, it is about the competing ideologies upon which alternative social policies for the provision of care for dependent people are based, namely familism and collectivism.

The development of community care policies

Care for dependent people – especially those who are infirm and very old – has become a live issue in the last two decades all over the developed world and is now becoming a matter of concern in developing countries as well. This is perhaps largely for demographic reasons, indeed the argument is always couched in these terms – but not wholly so. The reason why society chooses to focus on one set of problems as opposed to another at any given time is problematic and seems to have as much to do with the moral climate as with rational and pragmatic reasoning. The way in which that focus changes over time provides a valuable indicator of the values and assumptions upon which social policy and social action may be predicated.

The history of how society has treated those who are sick, infirm and dependent has changed over time. In Britain during the 1970s, for example, official rhetoric was on their side. The decade saw a spate of policy documents coming from central government exhorting the health and social services to give priority in services and resources to them (DHSS, 1976, 1977, 1981a). Professional and academic opinion came out strongly in defence of these client groups, arguing for more liberal and sensitive methods of handling them. The intention at that time was to shift resources from the acute sector of the health service towards what came to be termed the 'priority groups'. The 1970s and early 1980s were decades during which those policy intentions were played out with greater or lesser degrees of success. This was in contrast to a decade earlier, when official concern lay with unmarried mothers, institutionalized offenders and abortion seekers (Illsley, 1981) and the rediscovery of poverty, which commentators up until the 1960s thought had become a thing of the past.

Until the 1970s, the sick and the elderly as social categories had suffered a long history of being pushed to the bottom of the pile. This devaluing can be traced back to the nineteenth century (Pinker, 1979), a period that saw the workhouses gradually fill with sick and elderly people displaced or excluded from the voluntary hospitals. (There are grim parallels between this process and what has been happening to mentally ill people in recent years. More and more find themselves excluded from hospital care as the large asylums are closed, and instead find themselves thrown on to the unsympathetic mercy of the social security system and the streets.) As those hospitals began to develop as centres of curative medicine, teaching and research, the chronically sick were regarded as of little medical interest. The workhouse was the only place that would take them in. Similarly, during the Second World War, strategic planning to cope with large-scale civilian injuries decreed that elderly and chronically sick people should be moved out of the hospitals to make way for 'potential effectives', that is, injured but normally able-bodied civilians (Means and Smith, 1983). The argument implicit in those plans seemed to be that, *in extremis,* society dispenses with its responsibility to care for those who are weak and dependent, directing its efforts instead towards supporting those who are of potentially greater value to society in the long term. Revelations of the conditions since the war in which elderly, mentally ill and mentally disabled people have been kept demonstrate that little has changed even in recent times (Townsend, 1962; DHSS, 1971b).

Given this continuing history of disadvantage, it is perhaps remarkable that by the 1970s, official policy was beginning to give priority to these very groups. Why that should have happened is open to question, and various reasons have been offered (Illsley, 1981). It has been suggested that scandals and revelations about appalling conditions in long-stay institutions were the cause; it has also been suggested that at a time of economic recession, it is more socially and politically acceptable to focus concern on what society perceives as the 'morally blameless' categories of dependent people than on other, more 'suspect', groups. They are, such an argument would propose, morally blameless because they are in no way instrumental in their own misfortune. This is an important attribute when there is competition for social support. Just as during the nineteenth century the poor were seen either to be deserving or undeserving, so in recent years a number of disadvantaged groups have emerged, all vying for legitimacy in the eyes of society, all in need of society's support, and all in times of polarizing attitudes, tending to be set against each other and measured in terms of relative worth.

While the optimistic and relatively moralistically relaxed 1960s were prepared to widen the boundaries of what society perceived as deserving (hence the inclusion of offenders and unmarried mothers within those boundaries), times have subsequently changed and attitudes have become more judgemental. The hostile way in which people with HIV/AIDS have been treated by certain sections of society in recent years perhaps represents a redrawing of the moral boundaries. Those groups which in policy terms had until the recent past seemed invisible (older people, the infirm and disabled people) suddenly came to centre stage. Perhaps the reason for their acceptability in society's eyes was that their dependency, and hence their deservingness, was defined in medical terms; they were not perceived of as being morally responsible for their incapacity – in contrast with the other groups who are now seeking social support, namely, the able-bodied unemployed. As the waves of economic recession progressed during the 1980s and into the 1990s, there was a public rhetoric accompanying it which – flying in the face of the evidence – implied a degree of responsibility on the part of the unemployed themselves for their plight. Their moral worth was questioned through 'anti-scrounger' campaigns, political party discussion documents and speeches.

The then British prime minister, Mrs Thatcher, interviewed on television in February 1986, talked about her government's aim of getting people off the dole, back into (low paid and part-time) work, as 'getting them back into respectability and pride'. Peter Lilley, the social security minister, in his speech to the 1993 Conservative Party annual conference, took great delight in reading out a list of all those guilty of being undeserving that he would seek to penalize; 'scroungers' were high on his list. In the USA, the unemployed have been required to join workfare programmes in order to qualify for the dole, and in the 1990s various programmes have been introduced to force single parents into work and to penalize them if they have more children. Pilot schemes to pave the way for similar workfare schemes have been under consideration in Britain for some time. The academic community has taken up the cause. Charles Murray and others in the USA (Murray, 1984, 1990), and more recently a variety of British academics (Dennis and Erdos, 1992; Green, 1992), have started a vigorous debate about the 'underclass', arguing that the welfare state has been responsible for encouraging the growth of a class of people unattached to mainstream society – mainly single mothers, and young men who choose not to work and instead lead lives on the margins of society, living on benefits and deriving income through illegitimate means. Not only do the people who constitute the underclass *not* deserve society's support, but it would also be positively harmful to their long-term interests to give it to them – a convenient thesis indeed for those in power to avoid taking any responsibility for attempting to improve conditions for those at the bottom of the pile.

It is ironic that the abrasive moral climate that characterized the 'Thatcher years', with its emphasis on sturdy self-reliance and the ability of the individual to seek and find his or her own economic salvation, developed against a background of real economic decline and poverty. Not surprisingly in these circumstances, it was only those who fell within the newly and narrowly defined category of deserving who merited priority – largely those categorized as deserving through medical definition and who had long been so invisible. Even so, although the fact that they were categorized in this way conferred a certain amount of protection, it is disturbing to find in recent years that even these 'blamelessly' disadvantaged groups seem to be coming under attack from the political right. Rights to welfare benefits for disabled and invalid people have all come under scrutiny and have tended to be restricted or withdrawn. Changes to invalidity benefit, the main benefit for people off work through sickness, and to disability benefits were introduced in the 1990s, curtailing access rather than extending it (Rowlingson and Berthoud, 1994).

Thus it is debatable whether the declared priority has actually had any meaning in practice. Public statements have been made and the rhetoric constantly repeated, but the evidence over twenty years that ought to show a substantial improvement in the conditions in which dependent people find themselves is scant. The policies that were proposed twenty or more years ago to improve conditions envisaged the introduction of new types of care provision, with substantial transfers of resources from other sectors to finance them. The introduction of 'community care', as these policies came to be known, foresaw the closure of large-scale institutions that had traditionally housed those with mental health problems and those known as mentally handicapped people. These were to be replaced by small-scale 'homes', hostels, halfway houses and a variety of fostering arrangements for people who could not be returned to (or remain in) their own homes.

Community care policies had been taking shape since the 1950s, partly as a result of new drug therapies in the treatment of mental illness and partly because of new ideas being developed by a group of forward-thinking psychiatrists concerning the feasibility and efficacy of treating mentally ill people outside institutions (Archer and Gruenberg, 1982). They were later seized upon by planners who saw them as a means of cutting the high costs of caring for people in large institutions. The 1962 Hospital Plan (Ministry of Health, 1962) foresaw a massive reduction in the number of inpatients by the mid-1970s as a result of such policies. At the same time, the professions involved in caring for people with long-term needs adopted the same community-based approach. Institutional or residential care came to be regarded as the unacceptable face of state provision. The views of the professions were incorporated into government policy papers on the care of mentally handicapped and mentally ill people published in the 1970s (DHSS, 1971a, 1975). A consensus emerged between policy makers, planners, professional practitioners and academics about the acceptability of community care – a case of what Dunleavy has called 'ideological corporatism' (Dunleavy, 1981).

With the advent of the Conservative Government in 1979, official policy gradually began to focus on the role that families and individuals were expected to play within the framework of community care. The document on old age published in 1981 called upon traditional sources of support and stressed the centrality of the family as the bulwark of community care:

the primary sources of support and care for elderly people are informal and voluntary. These spring from the personal ties of kinship, friendship and neighbourhood... Care in the community must increasingly mean care *by* the community. (DHSS, 1981b)

As the decade wore on, it became increasingly apparent that the policy needed greater elaboration. Concern was developing about the way in which demands on the statutory services were growing in an unregulated way. The Audit Commission investigated community care provision in 1986 (Audit Commission, 1986); it concluded that there were serious grounds for concern about the lack of progress so far made towards shifting the balance of services towards community care and called for radical steps to be taken to improve the situation. Amongst these, it proposed that local authorities should be made responsible for long-term care for 'mentally and physically handicapped people' and that care of elderly people in the community should be funded from a single budget, no longer split between the NHS and local authorities.

Even more significant was the report by Sir Roy Griffiths, published in 1988 (Griffiths, 1988), which set out a framework for developing community care during the coming decade. It sought to harness the resources of the health and social services, along with those of the private and voluntary sectors, behind the concept of family-based care provided, wherever possible, in people's own homes. In making a clear distinction between health and social care, and confirming that health care alone should fall within the responsibility of the free-at-the-point-of-use NHS, it also raised the spectre of people having to pay for their care if they chose to look outside their immediate family and neighbourhood networks.

These trends were consolidated at the turn of the 1980s, following a series of White Papers (Department of Health, 1989a, b), in the NHS and Community Care Act 1990. Far-reaching changes to the organization and financing of the health service were introduced. The purchasing of services was vested in health authorities, while the provision of services was placed directly in the hands of newly formed trusts. This formed the basis of what was called an internal market, characterized by every service and episode of treatment being costed down to the level of the individual patient. Community care services became subject to the same sort of costing regimes, and the consequence of this has led to more and more people being expected to pay for community care services themselves. In addition, there has been a policy of transferring services from institutions to the community and, once they are in the community, transferring them to the responsibility of local authorities. According to official statistics, the number of hospital beds for elderly patients fell from 56 000 to 40 000 in the ten-year period from 1982 (Department of Health, 1994, Table 5.12).

Community care has thus become the centrepiece of current government health policy. Other aspects of the health reforms introduced in the 1990 Act are only able to be accomplished success-fully if community care begins to work effectively. This increasingly means that most older people, when they become infirm, will be expected to stay at home and be cared for there; for those with mental health problems, support will have to be found within the community or from within their own families.

Underlying much of the discussion about community care and the policies that promote it have been some fundamental assumptions about the nature and structure of family life, about the role of the family and the role of the state, and about the relative values of privacy, independence and interdependence. These are rarely made explicit and, where they are, they are simply stated as given. There has been little questioning of these basic premises or of the consequences to which implicit acceptance of them leads. In the next section, we shall examine some of these consequences, especially as they relate differentially to women and men.

The reality of community care: the consequences for carers and cared for

What then are the arguments against community care? On the face of it, the policy of giving dependent people a better quality of life, by taking them out of the frequently horrific institutional settings in which many had habitually lived, can hardly be criticized. Indeed, since so many of the big psychiatric institutions have now closed, it is becoming hard to remember the time when people with mental health problems were routinely incarcerated in such places. However, ever since the policies associated with community care were first introduced on any scale, there has been evidence that all has not been going well (House of Commons, 1985; Jones and Poletti, 1985).

Even as far back as 1961 there was evidence that the policy as it was being developed at that time was already faltering:

> At present, we are drifting into a situation in which, by shifting the emphasis from the institution to the community – a trend which, in principle and with qualifications, we all applaud – we are transferring the care of the mentally ill from trained staff to untrained or ill-equipped staff or no staff at all. (Titmuss, 1979, p. 109)

The criticisms and the evidence seem to fall into three categories. The first relates to the manner in which the policies are being implemented, while the others are related to the substance of the policies themselves and the principles upon which they are based.

The first set of criticisms is largely about political will and resources. They stress the fact that community care policies are failing to fulfil their earlier promise because there has been a failure of commitment at the highest level. This relates perhaps to the tensions inherent in the apparent consensus that underwrites the policies between planners, politicians and practitioners. Planners have tended, at least in the early days, to see community care as a way of saving on the heavy costs of institutional care; politicians have seen it as a means of demonstrating positive support for undervalued groups; practitioners have seen it as the most appropriate form of care from their clients' perspectives. While the latter have always insisted that satisfactory community care can only be achieved with huge injections of resources, planners and politicians have been less ready to concur (Dalley, 1989).

The 1985 Select Committee report (House of Commons, 1985) reviewed the progress made towards developing community care in the period since the publication of the landmark White Papers a decade before (DHSS, 1971a, 1975). It regretted the lack of progress and stressed the point that community-based services could not be established on a cost-neutral basis. It drew attention to similar mistakes made in the USA, where innovative thinking had promoted the development of community mental health centres but with inadequate resourcing, and in Italy where the policy known as *psichiatria democratica* had introduced major changes in some parts of the country but created problems in others. In both countries, the benefits and improvements had been patchy and piecemeal. Patients were discharged from long-stay hospitals only to find that there were not enough community facilities available. In the USA, the sight of ex-hospital patients living out of plastic bags on the streets became commonplace during the 1980s, and in Italy such patients began to find themselves being taken back into the hospitals that had discharged them – although these were now newly named as 'family homes', and the patients were referred to as 'guests'.

It was in the light of these criticisms that the Audit Commission (1986) and later the Griffiths Report (1988) looked closely at the problems associated with introducing community care. They both highlighted the slow and patchy progress that had been made and argued for greater commitment on the part of government, the NHS and local authorities towards ensuring its success. The Griffiths Report in particular made clear recommendations, in the name of greater effectiveness, about the need to separate responsibility for social care on the one hand and health care on the other, and to give local authorities the lead for implementing community care. These were to have profound implications for future policy developments, for it was partly on the basis of the recommendations made in the report that the legislative changes embodied in the NHS and Community Care Act 1990 were drawn up. It is this legislation that is governing current developments in community care in the mid-1990s, developments that have been roundly criticized by many of those charged with responsibility for providing it (NCVO, 1995).

As noted earlier, community care has, as part of major reforms to the health service introduced in the 1990 Act, become part of the internal market. NHS health authorities and local authority social services departments have been reconstituted as 'purchasing' authorities. Instead of providing services themselves as they did in the past, they are now required to purchase community care services from a mix of private and public sector providers. Charges for services have been introduced for the users of many of the services deemed to be providing 'social care', and the NHS has begun to withdraw from providing long-term health care in many areas, forcing people into dependence on the private sector and the financial charges that this involves. Thus one of the central planks of the welfare state when it was introduced in the period immediately after the Second World War – that of health care free at the point of use – has been substantially eroded. This is affecting many older people, who find themselves being obliged to go into private nursing homes, as hospitals will no longer care for them because the NHS is refusing to provide nursing home care itself and the people in question are too frail to be cared for at home. Even where there is the possibility of caring for them at home, local authorities are beginning to introduce substantial charges for domiciliary care, thus penalizing infirm and frail people who decide to, or are compelled to, stay at home.

In the case of people with mental health problems, many of the long-stay institutions have now been closed and the patients discharged. There is much debate about how far community-based alternatives have really become available to take the place of inpatient care and how far they have been successful (Leff, 1993). If the evidence from the streets can be relied upon, it appears that there are not enough. Hospitals talk about the 'revolving door', in which inpatients are discharged too soon after episodes of acute illness only to be readmitted because they cannot be cared for adequately in the community. In other cases, families complain about the extreme pressures they are under because there is not enough support available to help them care for family members who are unwell.

The policies then are finding little favour with clients and their families. This lack of acceptance links directly to the second category of criticisms concerning the nature of the policies themselves. There seems to be a fundamental assumption that the rationale underlying the policies – that is, of community-based forms of care – is appropriate to all forms of dependency. At first sight, the criticism is about quantity. If there were more community care, the problems would be solved. Just as all forms of institutional and residential care are, according to this view, perceived as unacceptable, so are all forms and conditions of dependency regarded as being amenable to care in the community. However, as the Select Committee report cited earlier stresses, there is still a need felt by many who are dependent for asylum, in the sense of haven or refuge, away from the stresses and rigours of the world. It may be that many of those stresses and rigours are caused by the prejudice and heartlessness of non-disabled people, and that those attitudes should be contested. It is hardly just, however, to expect the victims of that prejudice and heartlessness to fight that battle themselves from such an unequal and exposed position. It is important to recognize the needs and wishes of dependent people themselves. Practitioners and policy makers may be overly susceptible to what the Select Committee report calls 'the swing of the pendulum of fashionable trends and theories'.

This second set of criticisms relates, then, to the practitioner/ policy maker-defined nature of community care policies. It suggests that they are based on premises that do not necessarily correspond with the needs or wishes of all dependent people. The third category of criticism similarly questions the fundamental assumptions upon which the policies are based but this time looks at much broader-based assumptions, those underpinning wider social structure – the family and the position of women. At the root of all community care policies seems to be the firm belief that the family is the appropriate unit and location for care. Privacy and independence – both regarded as being goals to be prized and achieved – can best be secured by remaining in one's own home. The family, it is believed, has a moral duty to care. The bosom of the family is the place where a dependent person 'ought' to be. The state should keep out of the essentially private business of caring wherever possible. So the argument goes. Indeed, in 1995 the government seems to be taking this argument to its logical conclusion: the individual should look to the family for care; failing that, if the family cannot or will not care, the individual (and by extension the family through its economic relationship) must pay for care him or herself out of his or her own (family) resources (Department of Health, 1995).

It is clear that the playing out of community care policies is having major consequences for families, especially women, mostly as a result of the assumptions upon which they are based. Again, the report of the Select Committee, now more than ten years old, is a useful source of comment. It notes the heavy burden placed on the relatives of chronically dependent people and recognizes that the burden falls most heavily on the immediate family and on the mother in particular:

> despite this growing burden [on the immediate family], there is no evidence of any involvement by the wider community – friends, neighbours, volunteers or even extended family members – in providing any of the care which is needed from day-to-day. Instead, the burden of care falls largely on the young person's mother and results in marked financial, physical and emotional costs. (House of Commons, 1985, p. lxxxvi -vii)

The experiences recounted in the studies available at the time revealed the reality of community care policies for both carer and cared for alike (Wilkin, 1979; Equal Opportunities Commission,

1982; Glendinning, 1983; Ayer and Alaszewski, 1984). There was a pervasive lack of choice; the practical and conceptual distinction between 'care in' and 'care by' the community (Bayley, 1973) was meaningless. The professional services – hostels, group homes, home nursing, home helps, day care, respite care – which were envisaged by service providers as comprising community care, were even then proving insufficient, even where bolstered by voluntary organization support. The networks of neighbours, friends and extended kin perhaps helped on a sporadic and irregular basis (Abrams *et al.*, 1986) but rarely matched the expectations as defined as care *by* the community. Most often, care-giving devolved on to those closest to the dependent person – and those deemed to be closest were, and are, generally wives, mothers and daughters – or the dependent person was left to cope alone.

It is worth remembering that when that report came out, relatively little research had been conducted into informal caring. The following decade saw a burgeoning of interest in the topic (Twigg, 1992; Allen and Perkins, 1995). Much of it was concerned with examining the reality of caring for frail and infirm people at home (Ungerson, 1987; Hicks, 1988; Lewis and Meredith, 1988), showing what little support was available for both the person caring for and the person being cared for, and in doing so concentrated on describing the emotional and physical burden that was involved. The term 'carer' became a generally acknowledged designation; organizations such as the Association of Carers (later becoming the Carers' National Association) were established to further the interests of carers; central government funded information units (but not services) to provide support to carers (Dalley, 1993).

In the beginning, it was generally assumed, in a rather uncritical fashion, that the overwhelming majority of carers were women. They were assumed to be the 'women in the middle' (Brody, 1981), women usually of middle age, middle generation, between children and their own parents, who are prey to the competing demands of those children, those ageing parents and their own need to work (for whatever reason – be it financial or for satisfaction). This generalized view gave way to a more rigorous examination of the reality. Early examination of the data gathered in the General Household Survey (Green, 1988) showed that informal carers were a mixed category, with many men amongst them. The data showed that there were in the region of 6 million carers in the country, of whom 2.5 million

were men. Fifteen per cent of all women reported that they were
carers, 12 per cent of men reporting similarly. In the light of this
evidence, assertions that caring was predominantly a women's issue
came into question.

Further analysis of the data, however, sheds more light on the issue
(Arber *et al.*, 1988; Evandrou, 1990). The definition of 'caring'
employed in the survey was very broad, and most men reporting
themselves as carers fitted into the lighter end of the spectrum of
caring. Those who performed the heaviest tasks, for longer, of
personal care – washing, feeding, lifting – were, in the majority,
women, and the peak age group for caring was between 45 and 64
years, precisely the category pinpointed by Brody (1981). Other
research, however, has also demonstrated the extent to which caring
is also undertaken by older age groups – both women and, to a lesser
extent, men.

In a more recent study, this time an analysis of the 1990 census
data, relating to 2 700 adult informal carers, Arber and Ginn
confirmed the part played by men, finding that 10 per cent of men,
compared with 13 per cent of women, were undertaking some form
of caring. Men's caring was, however, generally less onerous, and they
tended to be men in later life, caring for their spouses. Women
tended to do more, more often and more intimately (Arber and
Ginn, 1995). As well as looking at the *amount* of caring that is
undertaken, researchers have continued to examine the *nature* of the
activity, both in relation to the emotional and physical sense (Wright
1986; Hicks, 1988) and in terms of the financial and economic costs
(Glendinning, 1992; Hancock and Jarvis, 1994; Parker and Lawton,
1994; Baldwin, 1995).

The exploration of the nature of care-giving and the dilemmas
for carer and cared for associated with it are discussed in the
following section.

The meaning of caring

Caring for and caring about

Exploring some of the many facets of caring is a difficult task; a
minefield of confusion seems to surround attempts to untangle the
concept. For example, at the affective level, a distinction can be made
between 'caring for' and 'caring about'. The first is to do with the

tasks of tending another person; the second is to do with feelings for another person (Parker, 1981; Graham, 1983). It is in the function of motherhood that the two processes most commonly coalesce, and it is from there, perhaps, that the problem of conceptual distinctions derives. It is considered perfectly natural that, in motherhood, caring for and about are so completely integrated that it is unnecessary to disentangle them; it is only when certain 'deviant' mothers choose to go against the norm and separate the two functions that any thought is given to the matter – and even then it is generally to reiterate that the two are indissolubly entwined. Caring for and caring about are deemed to form a unitary, integral part of a woman's nature (which cannot be offloaded in the 'normal' state of affairs). So if a mother decides to give up her child, even though she cares *about* it, to her divorced husband or for adoption, she is considered unnatural. Even if she chooses to maintain both the 'caring for' and 'caring about' roles but seeks to separate them (by handing over the 'caring for' to another person or agency on a temporary but regular basis), she is still regarded as deviant. Here her deviancy lies not in the denial of her nature (she still cares 'about' if not entirely 'for'); it lies, instead, in her attempt to split up the caring for and caring about functions. The two are deemed to be indissolubly linked.

This blurring of the boundaries between functions typifies woman's universe. In the domestic sphere, the menial tasks of family servicing are wrapped up and presented as part and parcel of her role as mother, and given the same affective value as the feelings she has about the family members for whom she is performing these tasks. Thus cleaning the lavatory and washing the kitchen floor are invested with as much significance (in relation to her devotion to and love of her family) as is reading a bedtime story to her child and being affectionate to her husband after a hard day's work at the office. It is a short step to transfer the same values to the tasks involved in servicing and tending family members outside the everyday cycle of family routine – when the child is sick or the husband incapacitated.

Some have suggested that the seeds of this confusion lie in the nature of woman's psychological make-up. However, Graham (1983) has rightly criticized the view that woman's nature, as characterized by psychologists (even feminists such as Chodorow), is about 'being' rather than about 'doing' (the essential characteristic of the male according to this view). Graham suggests that while this distinction may, in *practice,* characterize the difference between men and women, it is less to do with nature than with socially defined roles and arbitrarily drawn boundaries. However, in psychologists' terms, the 'caring about' nature of woman justifies the 'caring for' tasks that she performs. They are an expression of her essentially passive nature. In addition, it becomes the rationalization for women choosing work in the public sphere that is to do with 'caring for' people. Personal relationships become important; how often are schoolgirls heard to say, when talking about their future jobs, 'I want to do something with people.' This somehow justifies their entry into the otherwise 'forbidden' public sphere; it legitimates their break-out from the private sphere. For boys, on the other hand, it is perfectly legitimate to name 'career', 'money', 'success' as their concrete life goals.

The concentration of multiple functions in the role of motherhood seems to be at the root of the caring issue. Biological and social reproduction become confused: the function of bearing children (biological reproduction) and the emotional bonds that are associated with it become indissolubly linked with the tasks of servicing, maintaining and succouring the domestic group (social reproduction) within which childbearing takes place. It is then replicated in the public world (women's jobs service men's jobs, women's work relationships with men mimic their domestic relationships, and so on). Likewise, the role of mother in relation to her children is extended into other relationships and other contexts. In the 'extra-normal' situation of a child being chronically dependent beyond the constraints of dependency dictated by its age – through sickness and impairment – the mother automatically extends and is expected to extend her 'caring for' function. This then becomes the expected norm in relation to their non-child kinfolk in conditions of extra-normal dependency. Just as the affective links that form at birth are tied into the mechanical links of servicing and maintenance in the case of healthy children, the same affective links in the case of disabled and chronically dependent family members similarly get tied to the servicing and maintenance functions.

The effects of woman's caring role on the dependent person

In the public sphere, the same forces are at work; women go into the caring occupations because their natures and their intertwined capacities for caring for and caring about are thought to suit them well for those types of job. Evers (1981) describes how the mother role defines the model of care provided in certain hospital geriatric wards for frail and/or confused elderly people. The reversal of the mother–child relationship that frequently occurs when daughters look after their senile parents at home is mimicked in the institutional setting; fading old ladies are classified in childlike terms as good or naughty, difficult or compliant. A frequent complaint of adult disabled people is that they are regarded as children, simply because they are in wheelchairs, regardless of the fact that their intelligence and intellect are unimpaired. Ungerson (1983) draws attention to the ironically named radio programme *Does He Take Sugar?* as typifying this attitude: the disabled person's being ignored and the carer being asked questions about the simplest matters on his or her behalf.

The mixing of the caring functions (for and about) has implications for both parties in the caring relationship. Both find that the affective relationship of caring about each other becomes complicated by the overlaying of the 'caring for' relationship. Love, in this context, often becomes fractured or distorted by feelings of obligation, burden and frustration. However, the prevailing ethos of family-based care suggests that 'normal' tasks are being performed, that the roles enacted are straightforward, expected and unproblematic. The caring for of severely dependent people, especially adults, is, according to this view, simply an extension of usual family roles, but this is not necessarily so. Usual roles may have to be reversed, as described above, or the norms generally associated with incest prohibitions, together with conceptualizations about dirt and pollution, may be threatened and sometimes breached.

Ungerson (1983, 1987) describes a number of studies that focus on these issues, where daughters may be caring for mothers or fathers, or where fathers and mothers may be caring for adult daughters or sons. Thus the daughter having to care for a doubly incontinent father or a dementing mother, or a father having to cope with a mentally handicapped daughter as she starts her periods, for example, may all involve a transgressing of highly symbolic and significant social norms. Gender, age and sexual boundaries may all be breached, disturbing the sensibilities of all involved. However, because this model of family care is premised on the supposition that these are normal obligations to be fulfilled, many carers (and cared for) may develop feelings of guilt when they recognize that they themselves cannot accept these tasks as part of 'normal' family duty. Other evidence suggests that the boundaries of obligation and willingness are indeed carefully delimited – spouses are happy to care reciprocally for each other; this seems to be one of the implicit bargains of the marriage contract – but willingness to care for other dependents (and to be cared for) is highly relationship- and context-specific. As long as a disabled daughter or son is a child, caring falls within normal parameters (even though it may be arduous). Once the child becomes adult, tensions may develop in the caring relationship – love, obligation, guilt and dislike may all be intermingled.

The ambivalence frequently felt by those involved in the process of caring is made more problematic because public discourse insists that there can be no separation between caring for and caring about. Those who care *about* are expected always to care *for* and vice versa. Official and lay commentaries on community care policies all assert the conjunction of the two: chronically dependent people are best cared for at home or in home-like surroundings because this is the only location where the two processes coincide. Where the tasks of tending are not performed within the domestic group, by members (or a member) of it, there will be an absence of caring about. Conversely, where a woman cares about one of her dependants, she will always, so the public discourse propounds, care for them. This is always, it appears to be thought, a function of kinship relations; kinship relations are the essential precondition for the existence of the conjunction of the two processes. Furthermore, it appears to be specifically associated with a woman's capacity to care, bound up with the nature of woman as mother.

Men and the caring role

For men, the entanglement of caring for and caring about does not, broadly speaking, exist (and where it does, these men are usually regarded as atypical, in contrast to the case of women, where to *dis*entangle the processes is to be unnatural). Men, it is recognized, can care about without being expected to care for. The conjunction for men, rather, is to care about and thence to *be responsible for.* Thus a man who refuses to take responsibility for chronically dependent members of his family is regarded as callous and beyond the pale, but he is not expected to provide the care (that is, the tending) himself. He is expected to provide the setting within which the provision of care may take place (his own home, generally, with his own wife providing the care). However, if he has no wife, it is permissible for him to pay for the care to be brought in, or for the dependent person to be cared for elsewhere and/or to live elsewhere. The 'good son' is one who, typically, provides for his parents and/or other relatives financially (and supports his wife financially while she does the tending). The 'good daughter', in contrast, is one who 'sacrifices' herself (rather than merely her purse) and cares for her parents and/or other relatives herself.

There is evidence to suggest that in practice the official policies support this thesis. Several studies (Hunt, 1970; Blaxter, 1976; Levin *et al.*, 1985) have shown that chronically sick and disabled people are more likely to get a home help if they have a male carer to be responsible/care for them (and a disabled or chronically sick man is, in any case, more likely than a woman of the same condition to get a home help). Similarly, the way in which married and cohabiting women were excluded until the late 1980s from entitlement to the Invalid Care Allowance (a social security benefit for people looking after heavily dependent people) reflects official attitudes to the relative responsibilities of men and women. While these are examples of specific items of policy, the whole of community care policies can be seen to be based on the supposition that women are naturally carers, while men are naturally providers. Because such policies assume and presume the altruism of women, they reinforce that presumption. If no alternative forms of care or support are available, women will inevitably accept that it must be they who provide it. Whenever the policy documents talk about the responsibility, willingness and duty of families to provide care – *Growing Older* (DHSS, 1981b) being a good example – the substance of these statements is that they mean that *women* will do the physical and emotional providing for, while it is men who should underwrite this effort financially.

When the issue of informal caring arose as a matter for policy discussion in the 1980s, little factual information was available by which the assertions about the relative roles of women and men could be judged. As discussed earlier, when the first analayses of the Office of Population Censuses and Surveys data became available (Green, 1988), feminists were accused of overstating the case that women performed most of the caring involved. Although it is clear that these data show that men are involved in a substantial amount of caring, subsequent analysis has shown that the broad distinction outlined earlier between the different fields of responsibility shouldered by men and women is correct. Women are far more involved in the 'heavy' end of caring (Arber and Ginn, 1995), while men have lighter responsibilities and spend less time discharging them.

The consequences for women

What is the force that motivates women to accept the expectations of society at large that they should and will take on the caring function, at cost to themselves – all the evidence suggesting that the cost is great? The subordinate position of women in the domestic sphere seems closely bound to their role as carers of children and servicers of men, who are then able to restrict women's access to the public sphere where power, prestige and status are located. Where women do achieve access to that sphere, they start off with the handicaps of finding either that there are carefully constructed sidings of 'women's occupations' into which they are shunted – typified by their resemblance to women's work in the domestic sphere – or that they are regarded as atypical (and therefore abnormal) if they seek to achieve success in a male world on male terms – and they thus tend to be harrassed and put down, or given the status of honorary men.

The price women pay for subordination within the domestic sphere varies broadly according to class and education, although some features of it are common to all those who are mothers and servicers of men. Most of these women spend some years (whether many or few) confined to the home, looking after small children in isolation from other adults, with ideals of motherhood and house-craft to aim for which they find intolerably difficult to achieve. Levels of depression and instances of resorting to drug medication demonstrate how commonplace a problem this is (Brown and Harris, 1978). It was a central issue for women in the developing women's movement in the 1970s. For them it seemed to be a new phenomenon, a result of postwar society based on materialistic self-advancement, where individual nuclear families (husband out at work, mother at home rearing children) strove to improve themselves in competition with their neighbours and where success was measured in terms of material goods. The woman at home was expected to run her home efficiently (after all, hadn't she got all the labour-saving devices now?) and bring her children up successfully (which meant primarily that they should not make a mess in the house, since the smartness of the house – in imitation of the domestic environments portrayed in the burgeoning world of advertising – was a measure of family success).

However, it turned out to be a very lonely and unrewarding job; babies and toddlers were not made to be immaculate – their nature was to get dirty and be inquisitive, thus disrupting the smooth flow of housework. Housework itself was full of tedium; with every new labour-saving item on the market, standards continually rose. Instead of women being released from the relentless call of housework, they were given new tasks to perform. This was a new form of drudgery, and women who questioned it perhaps tended to forget the other sort of drudgery that their mothers and grandmothers had experienced in pre-Second World War days. Then the drudgery was much more tangible – years of endless childbearing, the loss of children, the physical toll wrought on women by endless pregnancies, heavy physical house-cleaning, washing and mending clothes. As the letters of working-class women collected by the Women's Co-operative Guild in 1914 demonstrate, this burden was frequently compounded by shortage of money and a need to cope with husbands' bitterness and frustration at lack of jobs or low wages. The letters are a fearful eye-opener to women born in the second half of the twentieth century (Margaret Llewelyn-Davies, 1978).

For some women, their lot as mother and housewife is and was made a lot easier through the privilege of class position, many tasks being made less arduous through their delegation to others (other women, of course). However, even so, there remains a remarkable fund of experience that is common to most women who are wives and mothers. Where women have gained access to the labour market – the public sphere – class position and levels of education have a more differentiating impact. Working-class women, with few skills or qualifications, are relegated to the monotonous 'dextrous' and 'mindless' occupations and to the lowest levels of the 'caring' occupations; they are low paid and work the double shift (home and work), with little outside assistance and little opportunity for advancement. For middle-class women with some educational qualifications, the opportunities are more diverse, but the problems of working women in male-dominated occupations are well known.

Thus in a society in which standards of success are measured in terms of the public sphere of male achievement and in which female work, both in and outside the home, tends to be dominated by routine, often physically onerous and, often, unrewarding activity, the cost that women pay is high. Why do women accept this cost? The common view is that it is located in women's special relationship to the function of caring, their capacity for self-sacrifice and their sense of altruism. The consequences of self-sacrifice are unfortunate in this view, but, because of the immutable nature of women's altruism, are inevitable. What is most remarkable is that women themselves seem to subscribe to this view of their nature and accept the structural consequences that stem from it. Thus it is not only men who hold this view, that is, those who are the beneficiaries of this set of assumptions, but also women, the chief losers in this conflict of interests, who subscribe to the same assumptions.

This raises the issue of ideology and the internalizing of values. A view that holds women to be caring to the point of self-sacrifice is propagated at all levels of thought and action; it figures in art and literature, it is the prop of official social welfare policies and it is the currency in which the social exchanges within marriage and the domestic sphere are transacted. It means that women accept the validity of this view as readily as men do. Once this central tenet – of women's natural propensity to care (in contradistinction to men's nature) – is accepted, the locus for that caring then becomes determined. With woman as carer, man becomes provider; the foundation of the nuclear family is laid. It becomes the ideal model to which all should approximate.

The nuclear family as ideal model

Ironically, though, this model is in *practice* less common than might be supposed. Most Western countries display a wide diversity of household composition (Family Policy Studies Centre, 1994). Britain, for example, shows this diversity. Some households may well be composed of nuclear families (that is, married couple plus dependent children) – about one third of all households in 1979; others (that is, the majority) are composed of a variety of forms – single parent, composite, single person, both young and old, and so on (Rimmer, 1981). By 1993, however, the proportion of households conforming to the 'traditional' pattern of a married or cohabiting couple with dependent children had fallen from 32 per cent in the early 1980s to 24 per cent (OPCS, 1993). The nuclear, individual-istic family is the reality for relatively few but the model for many.

The importance of this is in the consequence it has for those women who do not achieve the ideal. Of course, there is a category of bourgeois women who achieve both. For them, there is little contradiction between the ideal and the reality. The contradictions that they experience are perhaps more to do with an unarticulated disillusion with living lives as carers and servicers, unable to break free from the constraints of the domestic domain, unable to understand why achieving the ideal fails to satisfy them completely.

For most women, especially working-class women and women from ethnic groups, the contradictions are more obvious. The nuclear family is an essentially bourgeois structure and an ideological construct. As an expression of dominant values, it is placed before non-bourgeois women as the norm to which all should aspire, although many will inevitably fail. While bourgeois women who become feminists fight practically to 'get out from under' the *concrete* reality of the nuclear family form with all its associated values and prescriptions for behaviour, other women have to fight the form at a more abstract level. For working-class women, the model is a cruel irony. They have to contend with what Kollontai (1971) called the triple burden – childrearing, housework and wage labour; the prospect of shedding the latter burden in the manner of the bourgeois woman appears to be an attractive proposition. It is in the failure to achieve, but in wanting to achieve, the prescribed norm that working-class women are beset by contradictions. The past two hundred years have seen a progressive absorption into working-class consciousness of the ideological imperatives of the dominant, bourgeois, value system, of which the nuclear family ideal is a part. The task, from the feminist perspective, is for them to get that out of their heads, for them to escape the colonization of their minds.

Women from ethnic groups face a rather different set of contradictions, neither as a concrete form nor as an ideological construct does the nuclear family necessarily have meaning for them. It is part of the structure of the society into which they, or a previous generation, have been thrust, and as such it comes to symbolize their oppression. It is held as a model to which white, bourgeois society feels they *should* subscribe, but it is a model that perhaps has no basis, no roots in their own experience, consciousness or social forms. Their task, from the feminist perspective, is to resist this imposition, but also at the same time to question those ideologies of daily living that derive from the structure and culture of their own *milieux,* in the context of their own groups. They must determine for themselves how far those ideologies are acceptable to them as women and how far they are not. Of necessity, it is a task in which white women have very little part to play, apart from demonstrating the complementarity of their own struggle.

Internalizing values

The nuclear family and the roles associated with it, then, may not always exist in concrete form, but as an ideological construct, they are of crucial significance. Likewise, the ideological imperative of women's altruism that underpins it is also crucial. Land and Rose (1985) have discussed how fundamental to the ways of seeing women in modern society is the notion of altruism. They call the personal servicing that women do in caring for and caring about as *compulsory altruism,* encapsulating both the self-sacrifice and the selflessness involved *and* the prescriptive expectations of society that women shall perform that role. They look at the way in which strong women are portrayed in nineteenth-century novels as subordinating their own potential to the enhancement of male achievement (yet the authors themselves – George Eliot and Jane Austen, for example – were women who carved out a very independent role for themselves). Dorothea in *Middlemarch* is a classic example, commiting herself to the work of her husband Casaubon when it does not even merit it. However, it is not only in art that the ideal of the woman as self-subordinating and altruistic has held sway. Land and Rose show how social policies have been built on the same assumptions, to such an extent that the altruism that women come to see as naturally part of their character becomes compulsory. The policies could not be implemented, the structure would not function, if women declined to be altruistic. They cite both the Beveridge proposals and current community care policies as examples, suggesting that they reinforce the traditional pattern of enforced dependency and compulsory altruism. This is not, they argue, to be against the:

> expression of free altruism which potentially lies within community care and self help strategies... the feminist hostility to community care turns partly on the needs and interests of women which are to be masked once more in altruistic service to others and partly on the needs and interests of the cared for. In considering the needs and interests of *both*, feminists

accept a central insight from *The Gift Relationship.* Titmuss demonstrated
that for the gift to be safe, that is, non-injurious to the recipient, it had to
be freely given. (Land and Rose, 1985, p. 93)

This is the nub of the problem. To be critical of community care
policies is not to be critical of the importance of caring for and caring
about, or of the necessity of enabling disabled and dependent people
to live 'normalized' and 'ordinary' lives. Nor is it to deny that people
want to be cared for in familiar surroundings and to be cared about
by people about whom they themselves also care. However, because
there is consensus at the level of public discourse (both official and
lay) that community care is the right policy, both on ethical and
pragmatic grounds, feminists run the risk of being severely criticized
as self-interested and uncaring. It is important that they contest these
judgements: to fight for women's rights is to fight for justice, just as
it is to fight for the rights of any disenfranchised, subordinated or
devalued group; to question the nature of community care is to seek
solutions that are equitable, comfortable and acceptable for dependent people as well as for women as (potential) carers.

For the moment, there is widespread acceptance of the way things
are. Women have internalized the altruistic ideal; society has capitalized on it. With women being prepared to remain or return to the
home to care, society is provided with a ready-made 'reserve army' of
nurses, an army that does not need hospitals to be built for it to work
in and does not need wages to be paid it, because, *it is assumed,* its
members are already provided for by being dependent on, and thus
supported by, wage-earning men. It is this 'reserve army' that is
increasingly being activated to provide the community care that
policies and politicians have been calling for over recent years, a form
of care that is largely uncosted and unmeasured, which can be
invoked by planners and politicians without its cost being borne by
official resources. Women are offered little option as to whether they
participate as carers or not.

Indeed, choice is certainly not available to those in need of care. To
those in long-stay institutional care, the future offered is a disconcert-
ingly vague promise of care at home, if it is available, or some form of
supported living in a quasi-home (a hostel, group home or halfway
house). However, the reassuring security of 'asylum' is not there, and
after many years out of mainstream society, reintroduction into
society, often at the most painful entry points (the world of the

destitute, homeless and workless), is harsh and difficult to cope with. For those who would formerly have entered long-term care, older people in particular, the closure of such facilities by the NHS frequently means expensive care within the private sector or no care at all.

This, then, is the all-too-frequent reality of community care. In the following chapter, we shall examine the ideologies of familism and possessive individualism that seem to lie at the heart of that reality.

2

Familist ideology and possessive individualism

The ideology of familism

Before taking the discussion about ideology any further, it is perhaps necessary to clarify what is meant by the term in this context. It was discussed earlier how a particular view of the family and the expected roles of its various members underlies a whole range of policies, especially, but not exclusively, policies related to caring. There is a consistency and a patterning in this that suggests a coherent ideology underlying these social forms. Fallers (1961) defined ideology very broadly as 'that part of culture which is actively concerned with the establishment and defence of patterns of belief and value'. This definition, while it omits discussion of establishment 'how' and 'in whose interests', does stress the *defence* of these patterns, which emphasizes that ideology is something that is contestable. Thus dominant ideology is that which successfully establishes and defends its hegemony, overriding others' interests and buttressing those which it underpins.

In the present discussion, it is the ideology of familism – or familialism, as Barrett and McIntosh (1982) have termed it – that has established its dominance and operates as a principle of social organization at both the domestic and public levels, especially in the field of social care. This has major implications for the position of women. As an ideological construct, 'the family' – the central focus of familism – underlies all contemporary forms of social organization of daily living. This does not mean that all such forms are conscious or unconscious approximations of the construct, but it is the standard

26

against which all forms are measured and, importantly, judged. Thus within, and according to, the ideology of familism, non-family forms are deemed to be deviant and/or subversive. Also, it is argued, because of the hegemonic nature of familism, assorted categories of individuals subscribe to, or have internalized, the values of that ideology even though its dominance may, objectively, run counter to their interests. If they fail to achieve the required standard, they may then perceive *themselves* as deviant. The pull exerted by the ideology of familism is demonstrated in the call by the British government in the early 1990s to return to traditional family values as the solution to a range of social evils – juvenile crime, marital breakdown, single parenthood, ill-discipline in schools and more.

The fourfold application of familism

Taking the ideology of familism as a starting point, an explanatory model can be constructed that accommodates a parallel pair of replications – one reproduced internally (within the domestic group) and the other externally (in the public sphere). Thus the principles underlying the social organization of daily living (as demonstrated in patterns of residence, household membership, the domestic division of labour and relationships of domination and subordination) are replicated in the caring functions performed by that group (through the social organization of care, provision for children and other dependent members of the group, the altruism and self-abnegation typically expected of women and the manner of the social construction of dependency).

This internal pattern of replication is then reproduced in the public sphere; the ideology underpinning domestic relations becomes a major organizing principle upon which social relations outside the domestic group are based. It governs major and fundamental cleavages between the public and private spheres, creating a gendered division of labour in which women are, for the most part, principally consigned to the private sphere, although being drawn out into the public sphere according to the demands of the market or when they are of intermediate status (single, or non-mothers, that is, when they do not 'fit' the ideological premise of women as biological reproducers and social servicers). Or they may be marginal, peripheral workers, working part time to augment the inadequate 'family wage' earned by the male breadwinner. Beyond the private/public division, within the public sphere itself, the ideological principle also governs social relations: men's careers are structured on the premise that women will provide the servicing functions that allow men to pursue their career interests single-mindedly; certain female occupations reproduce the familial subordination/dominance model in relation to 'male' occupations – nurses/doctors, secretaries/bosses, and so on. Even though work patterns have been changing quite substantially in the closing years of the twentieth century, the underlying ideological impulse remains largely unchanged. We find it hard to accept and adapt to these new patterns as they emerge, focusing only on the problems that they throw up instead of capitalizing on the benefits that the breaking down of old traditions may offer.

Just as the ideology supporting domestic organization also validates the organization of care-giving domestically, that same ideology reproduced in the public sphere of work and public affairs is also replicated in the field of social care. This can be demonstrated by examining policies designed for the public provision of care for dependent people (both adults and children), and by looking at the position of women who, by implication, figure largely in those policies as carers.

This cluster of replications is well known; modern feminists over the past twenty years and more have demonstrated how the whole of domestic life is premised on the unequal division between men and women. Patterns of residence fragment and isolate individuals into small domestic units, dependent on the individual servicing of the household by women as wives and mothers; houses and flats are built only for such small units. The legal conditions under which residential accommodation is leased or mortgaged has tended, at least until relatively recently, to recognize this family group as the accepted unit of residence. Within the domestic unit, the division of labour is sharply drawn, as research studies have shown (Oakley, 1974). In spite of media discussion in the 1990s of the arrival of the 'new man', apparently willing to participate more equally in the domestic sphere, he has not so far made a convincing appearance. Relations of domination and subordination prevail; studies of domestic violence suggest that physical violence is less rare than defenders of the familial form would claim (Dobash and Dobash, 1980). Rather than its being an aberrant form of family life, it is perhaps an inevitable consequence of the structure itself.

Another aspect of subordination is manifested in patterns of resource allocation within families. Pahl (1980) has shown how frequently women receive unequal shares of family income, restricted by their menfolk's budgetary control. How much money the woman receives frequently depends on his whim, yet more often than not it is she who is expected to provide for the family. Child allowances paid directly to the woman may well be the only source of income that a woman can lay claim to, hence the importance, past and present, of campaigns to make sure that such allowances are preserved. The limitation of wives' rights to a share in their husbands' occupational pensions once they are divorced is further evidence of the subordinate economic position women occupy in relation to men.

Intimately bound up with women's role within the domestic unit is their role as carers. The biological divisions of gender difference are again capitalized on. Thus men accumulate not only power and access to the public sphere, but also the servicing power of women. Their children (and by extension their other dependants) are cared for by their women; childcare within the home is favoured and supported by expert opinion. Bowlby (1953) and Leach (1979) are widely cited by those favouring the home-centredness of women, suggesting that young children will suffer if separated from their mothers too soon. Even where integration of the child into an external social world is favoured, the child, it is argued, should be accompanied by its mother. There are many preschool activities (the British Pre-school Playgroup Association groups being an example), taken up especially by middle-class mothers, that are structured precisely on the full participation of mothers as well as children.

Women are expected to provide care not only for their immediate dependants (their children and their ageing parents), but also frequently for their husbands' ageing dependants (that is, their parents-in-law). If they do not marry, they are expected to give up participation in the public sphere of work and look after their dependent relatives alone. The National Council for the Single Woman and her Dependants (renamed the National Council for Carers and their Elderly Dependants in 1982, subsequently becoming part of Carers' National Association) did not refer to the single woman without good reason. Indeed, in the case of the unmarried woman, rather than her being subordinate to a husband as in the case of her married sisters, she remains subordinate to the demands and expectations of her family of birth. Thus her single status does not confer any real independence from familial, domestic responsibility; there always remain latent demands on her freedom, that can be activated at time of crisis.

Thus in the private or domestic domain, there is a twofold, unequal division between women and men, first, in the social organization of daily living, and second, in the social organization of care-giving. This internal replication is then produced in the public sphere. In the external or public sphere of work, the division of labour, whereby women are excluded from certain sectors, concentrated into others or relegated to lowly status in yet others, is a reflection of the pattern of relations within the domestic unit, where women are largely concerned with servicing and maintenance roles and are frequently excluded from equal access to family resources. Men's work, for example, has traditionally been organized on the presumption that their wives will provide supportive assistance – there is a literature (for example, Finch, 1983; Callan and Ardener, 1984) on the incorporation of women into their husbands' work. The clergyman's wife is an example. Large companies and political parties have been known to vet men's wives to ensure their suitability in this supportive role. Where women work in the public sphere, they are frequently concentrated in 'female' occupations, for example, the 'caring' occupations, such as nursing, social work, teaching and health auxiliary work, which all depend on the supposed instinctive caring capacities of women; or the 'dextrous' occupations, such as small-scale electrical assembly work, which depend on the supposed innate aptitude of women to do intricate, complicated, manual work; or the 'mindless' occupations, such as monotonous repetitive conveyor belt work, packing and cleaning, which depend on the supposed disinclination of women to apply themselves to intelligent forms of activity. The evident diversity of these three 'innate' female characteristics is rarely noted.

Familial ideology affirms these forms; it affirms that there is indeed something natural and appropriate about women's place being predominantly in the domestic sphere, that they have a natural inclination towards and aptitude for performing the monitoring, servicing tasks within the family setting. Furthermore, it affirms as natural the dominance of men within the private sphere and, inevitably, in the public sphere, over which they have, or should have, it is believed, near monopoly of access.

Caring is perceived of as one of the integral functions of the domestic group so depicted; the caring for and socializing of children is seen as correctly taking place within the domestic sphere, and it is a small step to extend this function of caring to include the caring for of other dependants, the chronically ill and disabled family members of all ages. This, of course, presupposes the continuous presence (or activation of such a presence when necessary) of the woman in the family.

Where the private function of caring breaks down and the public sphere takes on responsibility for the provision of care (which it has done on more than a residualist basis for centuries), the same ideology of familism is now reproduced. It is a mark of the hegemonic nature of familial ideology that, in recent years, it has become the foundation of public policy for care as well as of private care, at a time when the actuality of family *structure* has been demonstrated to be a fluid and shifting form (Rimmer, 1981; Gittins, 1985; OPCS, 1993; Family Policy Studies Centre, 1994). Social care replicates, or is expected to replicate, the family form of care as closely as possible.

Policies relating to the care of those patient groups designated as 'priority groups' in current health service policy documents exemplify this; they are based on a normative framework of 'family care as best'. This has two aspects: first, that for dependent individuals care is best provided for 'at home', and second, that for the kinfolk of those dependent individuals, there is an overriding moral duty for them to provide that care. The policies are consciously articulating the ideology of familism: in recent years there has been a publicly achieved consensus between policy makers, practitioners and 'experts' from the academic world that the family model of care is the appropriate policy goal, and that it is one that should be applied in all fields of dependency. It has figured prominently in the deinstitutionalization debate, so that the revulsion rightly felt towards the grossest examples of dehumanized institutional care has been directly linked with the view that the appropriate alternative in all cases is family-based care. Where that form of care is not available, measures that are 'nearest approximations to that form' are introduced. An associated ethos of 'rights to surrogate family care if "own family" is unavailable' is fostered to legitimate these measures (Dalley, 1983). Propounders of the familist ideal favour it because it embodies for them notions of the family as haven, as repository of warm, caring, human relationships based on mutual responsibility and affection, and thus a private protection against a cold, hostile, outside world.

The practical and unfortunate consequences of familism

Policies that enshrine these assumptions have consequences both foreseen and unforeseen. Amongst the foreseen are the direct consequences for women. They are the individuals expected to be available for caring. If dependent people are to be decanted from institutions into the community, back to their homes, there have to be people available to care. Caring in the community is regarded as a domestic function; women, according to the ideology of familism, form that category of individuals that pertains to the domestic sphere. Therefore it is a given that it is they who will do the caring. In practice, however, given the diversity of family and household structure, there may not be enough women available to provide the necessary care.

Thus the family model of care becomes infinitely flexible; it becomes the rationale for the dementing old lady being maintained in her home, living alone, perhaps with few relatives who might be able to visit or, more importantly, perform caring tasks. She is supported by a variety of professional services, coming in on a daily (or less frequent) basis – district nurse, health or geriatric visitor, GP, social worker, home help, meals-on-wheels deliverer, to name the most likely – all of which confusion serves to exacerbate her dementia. Or perhaps she may be bussed to the local psychogeriatric hospital for the day, returned at night to 'her familiar surroundings', locked in alone, until sometime the next morning the ambulance arrives again, to repeat the exercise, removing her to a more monitored environment. This care is called 'care in the community'; the fact that the woman sleeps in a bed in her own home at night is deemed to represent own-home care. At the other end of the scale, harrassed health authorities close down large psychiatric hospitals or the geriatric wards of district hospitals only to build sixty-, seventy- or eighty-bed units on the same sites, often behind the same high walls, and call them 'homes', 'home-like' or 'community units'.

The same rationale is also used to justify the apparently endless moves of children in care from one foster family to another, interspersed by return to the family of birth and indeterminate lengths of stay in children's homes (regarded as the most inappropriate forms of care, because they are 'institutions'). Equally, it becomes the justification for the return of children from care to parent or parents who live in isolation, lacking support from networks of kin or friends, and who present real threats to the physical and emotional well-being of their offspring.

At a more insignificant level, middle-class mothers, especially in the affluent south-east of England, turn to mother substitutes to care for their children. From *The Lady* (a monthly magazine for the genteel English middle classes) to the notice board in the corner shop, there are advertisements searching for either unemployed school-leavers, qualified nannies or homely 'motherly' ladies to care for the babies, toddlers and preschool children of the middle classes. Substitute mothers are preferred over the alternative – collective childcare in nurseries or nursery schools – because it mimics most closely the family model of care.

Thus the justification in all these examples is that the solution to the problems of care must be based on approximations to the family model of care. Rather than the particular needs of particular patient or client categories being examined in their own terms, satisfaction of those needs is forced into a single mould labelled 'community care', whether or not the measures decided upon are appropriate. Similarly, the outcome of such measures frequently turns out to be inappropriate. Frail and confused elderly people live isolated and bewildered lives, out of contact with their peers and their kin; young children are moved from one setting to another lacking the very security and familiarity the policies were, apparently, designed to foster; the favoured sons and daughters of the middle class are often cared for by bored and frequently exploited teenagers who have little idea of the basic requirements of childrearing; community-based hospital care develops rapidly into the institutional form of care it was intended to replace.

There are further consequences. Alternative forms of care are denigrated or declared redundant. Old people's homes, hospital-based continuing care provision and children's homes all become the focus of professionals' and policy makers' attack. Furthermore, the occupants of this form of care become stigmatized along with the residential units that accommodate them. People dependent on a long-term basis, either through old age, youthful infirmity or disability, become identified with the form of care provided; the people providing that care take on some of the stigma too. Care-workers in institutional settings tend to be low-paid, lacking in qualifications, often of low morale and undervalued.

These, then, are some of the consequences of the penetration of familist ideology into so many levels and areas of social organization. But why should that penetration be so all-embracing? How has this state of affairs come to be? It seems inevitable that answers have to be looked for in the past. It is clear that this tradition of familism has been firmly established for many generations. We are familiar with the expectations of 'womanly behaviour' as laid out in nineteenth-century literature; the idealized nuclear family model has been with us for many years. Its values and the goals it is said to stand for are clearly linked to those of a wider philosophical tradition – possessive individualism. This relationship will be explored next.

Possessive individualism and its relationship to familist ideology

Possessive individualism incorporates a number of related notions: the individual as an 'independent centre of consciousness' in Kant's terms, the notion of the self and self-determination, of privacy and freedom from intrusion. Along with these is the quality of possessiveness, which is found 'in the conception of the individual as essentially the proprietor of his [sic] own person and capacities, owing nothing to society for them... The human essence is freedom from dependence on the will of others, and freedom is the function of possession' (Macpherson, 1962, p. 3).

In this vision of the autonomous proprietorial individual, one thing is clear – that individual is male. Women and children become 'owned', just as the individual 'owns' himself. In this way, man and his appendages (woman/wife and children) are one in relation to notions of autonomy and privacy: a woman has no autonomy; she is merely a part of her husband's autonomy. Thus great emphasis is placed on the autonomy and privacy of the *family unit* (man, wife and children) as a buttress against the intrusion of outside institutions, notably the state. Freedom of action within the family is cherished – freedom to amass wealth, to own property, to dispose of it as the family chooses, to pass name and property on to the children. Sets of opposed interests are constructed. Some are external – the family against the state, the family as distinct from other families, private (family) property as opposed to collectively owned property – whereas others are internal – parents in control of children, husband in ascendancy over his wife. After all, an English*man*'s home is his castle, as the saying goes. The nuclear family is clearly a key element in all this.

The development of the nuclear family form and its underlying ideology has been accounted for broadly in two different ways, On the one hand, some have suggested that it has its origins in the idiosyncratic nature of English society, going back at least to the medieval period. On the other hand, others have said that it owes its origins to the advent of capitalism and the consequent split between domestic and productive forms of labour.

The historical origins of the nuclear family

The 'idiosyncratic' argument suggests that, in the English context, it is too simplistic to argue that there was a classical transition from peasant economy, based on communal enterprise (with identity of interest focused on the extended family and village, where the extended family group operated as a combined production, reproduction and consumption unit), to capitalist economy, characterized by a split between domestic and productive labour, and a fragmentation of interests between the owners of the means of production and the wage labourers. According to Macfarlane (1978), for example, the classical peasant economy – typified by communal landholding vested in the family as a whole rather than the individual head of the family, strong legal and sentimental attachment to the land, close-knit 'organic' village communities jealous of outside intrusion, and the large, kin-based household as a unit of production and consumption – was not typical of English socio-economic organization, certainly from at least the thirteenth century. His examination of contemporary documents demonstrates a high degree of geographical and social mobility, small household size and high levels of wage labour (between 50 and 70 per cent of the population being defined either as servants or wage labourers) and an active market in land (rather than its being vested in perpetuity within the continuing extended family, as the classical peasant model presupposes). He concludes that the majority of English people were already, by that time, 'rampant individualists, highly mobile both geographically and socially, economically rational, market-oriented and acquisitive, ego-centred in kinship and social life' (Macfarlane, 1978, p. 163).

The findings of Laslett and the Cambridge population studies group relating to household size and structure support the Macfarlane hypothesis. They suggest that in medieval times households were based on the conjugal union of husband and wife, together with their offspring, and that first marriage took place at a later age than that typically associated with peasant economies and joint landholding (Laslett and Wall, 1972). They see the medieval family as 'embryonically' modern in form, just as Macfarlane does. To these writers, the 'family' was essentially defined in kinship terms and bounded by co-residence – those kin living under one roof, related by blood and marriage.

In contrast, however, for writers such as Flandrin (1979), the term 'family', especially the aristocratic family, was not simply a kin-based unit, although it *was* a residential unit. It referred to all members of the household, whether or not related by blood and marriage, thus including servants and other associated non-kin. This, of course, is reminiscent of the Roman meaning of 'familia', which was originally a household of slaves, only later coming to mean all members of the household – blood and affinal kin, together with servants and slaves. When the medieval households to which Laslett and Macfarlane refer are examined, it is clear that they frequently contained substantial numbers of unrelated individuals, albeit clustering around a nucleus of conjugally defined kin. They are convinced that the evidence they have produced confirms their view that, from the Middle Ages onwards, the central feature of English social structure was the individualistic nuclear family, within which property and inheritance rights were vested and production and consumption were based.

Greer (1985), however, criticizes the view that co-residence was a crucial factor in the defining of 'the family'; kinship-relatedness and the content of those relationships is for her the true defining factor. Thus, she argues, Laslett may be correct in concluding that many households did not contain extended family groups, namely kin-relatedness extending beyond the conjugal unit plus offspring, but what his 'curiously unreal' census figures do not take into account is the fact that the *reality* of kinship ties (social, emotional and economic support) is not necessarily limited by the factor of residence. In addition, she questions how far census data relating to family details are accurate, for 'peasant families are seldom anxious to tell the whole truth to bureaucratic authorities, even when they

think in terms that bureaucracies can grasp, which they seldom do'
(Greer, 1985, p. 231). Others would argue that place of residence
was crucial, since that determined the unit of production and
consumption and the boundaries of economic responsibility towards
kin (R. M. Smith, 1984).

Of course, Greer is contesting the view that the nuclear family has
been the norm since bygone days. She is suggesting, on the contrary,
that it is a recent and aberrant form of social organization, limited to
white, Protestant, north-west Europe and the USA. However,
Macfarlane's view is that, quite apart from the demographic structure
of households, enough is known about landholding practices, legal
rights (which gave women substantial rights) and other practices, to
conclude that there was a form of domestic organization based on
the individualistic nuclear family that predated the development of
capitalism. Greer is undeterred by such assertions; the argument put
forward by Mount (1981) in *The Subversive Family* is another lamb
to the slaughter. He suggests that the nuclear family has existed and
persisted for centuries in spite of relentless attacks on it from
dominant interests of all sorts. However, Greer turns his argument
on its head. Rather than its being the nuclear family that has
persisted throughout the centuries, despite attacks on it from every
direction, as Mount argues, it is the *extended* family, or the Family, as
Greer refers to it, that has survived down the ages. Although increasingly under pressure from those who preach the 'doctrine of instant
gratification', which she sees as being part of the destructive forces
that the Western world is bringing to bear on 'traditional communities' all over the world, it continues its struggle to survive.

Greer stands in opposition to those such as Macfarlane and Laslett
who see the nuclear family as having a long historical past, but she
does not quite fit the category of those who seek to locate the rise of
the nuclear family in the advent of capitalism. Like the latter, she
suggests that it is a recent form and that the extended family (in this
sense, any grouping of kin more elaborate than the conjugal unit of
husband and wife plus offspring) predated it. However, while they
perceive the crucial cleavage as being historically grounded between
precapitalism and capitalism, Greer sees it more as lying between 'the
western world' and 'traditional communities', that is, a cultural
cleavage, since traditional communities may be villages in rural Italy
or India (neither of which are precapitalist), while the Western world
is that set of urban, sophisticated, consumerist ideas and attitudes

encountered the world over, rather than being a geographical or historical entity. She is perhaps arguing that the extended family derives from a different philosophical tradition, which is in direct contrast to the possessive individualism that is the progenitor of the nuclear family form.

While all three approaches agree with the Macfarlane view that the nuclear family is structured on a foundation of individualism, those who see it firmly linked to the development of capitalism argue that it has its conceptual foundations in the thought of the Enlightenment, rather than its being a feature of the English character throughout the centuries. Hardy (1981) suggests that the seventeenth-century political theorists were probably only forging into philosophical thought that which had been the 'actual assumptions of middle-class English people over four or more centuries'. Lukes (1973) has summarized the main tenets of this thinking: the principle of the 'intrinsic value and dignity of the individual human being', the notion of autonomy, whereby the 'individual's thought and action is his own and not determined by agencies or causes outside his control', and privacy – that 'private existence within a public world, an area within which the individual is or should be left alone by others and able to do and think whatever he chooses' (the female gender, apparently, is rarely used in philosophical discourse). Lukes also describes two further elements as constituting individualism – self-development and a view that individuals form society as 'independent centres of consciousness, generating their own wants and preferences in a rational manner'. Thus individualism is seen as being the ideological foundation upon which the transition to capitalism was based. Within that process, it was the notion of the bourgeois family that encapsulated the ideology of individualism most perfectly.

The bourgeois family

Central to the notion of the bourgeois family and its individualistic philosophy, is the subordinate position into which women are placed. Socialist–feminist and Marxist analyses pinpoint the separation of domestic labour from productive labour in the capitalist process as the crucial determining factor in the modern segregation and subordination of women. Secombe (1974), for example, suggests that in the precapitalist period, the domestic domain was conterminous and sometimes indistinguishable from the productive sphere; and although others have argued that women under pre-capitalist formations were already consigned to the domestic domain, with an already gender-based division of labour (what Marx calls the 'natural division of labour') established within the 'feudal family', they nevertheless assert that the household economy was in general characterized largely by common productive labour· for the benefit of the family unit as a whole.

Barrett, however, warns against the danger of idealizing the 'feudal family' as a social form in which women did not suffer the segregation and domestication that they were later to experience under capitalism. She suggests that 'it might be more useful instead to consider ways in which pre-capitalist gender divisions have been incorporated, possibly entrenched and exaggerated into the structure of capitalist relations of production' (Barrett, 1980, p. 181).

Although there may be disagreement, or at least a certain lack of clarity about the state of gender relations and particular family form in the precapitalist period, most sources agree that the advent of capitalism heralded the development of a new role for women as reproducers. In contrast to the earlier period, domestic labour now became responsible for the social and biological reproduction of a form of labour power that was to become engaged in wage labour and the production of surplus value for the employer. However, although this reproductive role is crucial, it was, and is, rendered invisible by the way it has been socially constructed. The reproductive/servicing role of women within the family, in relation not only to those already engaged in productive labour and those who will be in the future, but also to those who can no longer function as such – the chronically sick and the aged – has consistently been taken for granted and relegated to the private, personal sphere. It has thus remained sociologically and politically unanalysed until the advent of the feminist critique.

The family form characteristic of capitalism indicates a structure in which the division of labour according to gender is clearly defined, as between domestic and productive labour. But where does individualism, the ideological foundation upon which this new family form was structured, fit in? The family form, as described, is that of the wage labourer; the family form that rests upon the bedrock of individualism is essentially the bourgeois family, certainly nuclear in structure (husband, wife and children), but one that is more concerned with the amassing of wealth and private property than being engaged in selling the labour power of its members in the marketplace.

This confusion is rarely resolved in discussions of the historical development of family forms. Clearly, the major change in the mode of production, which is the defining characteristic of capitalism, caused the fragmentation and separation of production, reproduction and consumption. A discrete domestic domain was, probably for the first time, created throughout society, affecting bourgeoisie and proletariat alike – and this was created by the removal of production from the domestic domain (although home-working confuses the picture) and not because women were segregated and consigned to that domain (because that had always been the tendency). (Although, conceptually, many feminists would argue that it is incorrect to draw a sharp and absolute distinction between public and private, because in reality they 'interpenetrate' each other, it is still useful analytically to draw the *broad* distinction between them.) The principles of individualism are embodied in the ideals and aspirations conventionally assigned to the bourgeois family: the single-minded pursuit of self (family)-improvement, both in material and spiritual terms, and the determination that the family, under the guidance of the head of the family – the husband/father – should be autonomous in thought and action, especially in relation to the upbringing and education of its children. The Bergers summarize it thus:

> an emphasis on high moral standards, especially in sexual matters; an enormous interest in the welfare of children, especially their proper education, the circulation of values and attitudes conducive to economic success as well as civic peace; at least the appearance of religious faith; a devotion to the 'finer things' in life, especially the arts; and last but not least, a sense of obligation to redress or alleviate conditions perceived as morally offensive. (Berger and Berger, 1983, p. 17)

While these ideals and aspirations were far removed from the reality of life, as experienced by the exploited and oppressed newly urbanized working class throughout the nineteenth century, the Bergers argue that, gradually through time, the concept of the bourgeois family first as a sort of 'ideal type' and later as a reality has been taken over by the working class. In fact, they argue, this has happened to such an extent that it is now the working class that defends the principles upon which the bourgeois family form is founded, while what they term the new 'knowledge class' consistently seeks to subvert and overturn them.

Marxists would suggest that this is a case of the subordinate class absorbing and taking on the values of the hegemonizing dominant class. Certainly the contrast between working-class life and attitudes in nineteenth-century Britain, as depicted, say, by Engels and Mayhew, and that of the present day is strong. Bourgeois ideals of marriage, the careful upbringing and education of children and the cultivation of a private domain of diligent self-improvement were far from the experience of the most down-trodden sections of the working class in Victorian Britain. In marked contrast is today's working class, from which a substantial amount of support in recent years has been drawn in both Britain and the USA for the right-wing values of sturdy self-reliance and for a rejection of what Margaret Thatcher famously called 'moaning minnie' welfarism.

While Marxists would regard this as an outcome of false consciousness, the Bergers applaud the bourgeoisie's colonization of working-class value systems. They see the cleaving of the working class to the bourgeois values of individualism, as embodied in the nuclear family, as the means of preserving what is best in modern Western society, preserving what they call 'the middle ground'. They expound at length on the manner in which the present-day working class has taken on the attitudes formerly espoused by the bourgeoisie – and indeed regard these new working-class attitudes as a bulwark against the encroachment of more subversive values. In their view, the modern professionals (social workers, therapists and teachers) who are the heirs of the nineteenth-century philanthropists and bourgeois 'good women' now police the working class in the name of values that are anathema to the old ethos of self-determination, self-reliance and family integrity. For the Bergers, it is necessary to take power away from such professionals and reinvest it in the hands of those best suited to hold it – honest, decent, hard-working parents. They cite professional attitudes to the role of women in the home as an example of what has gone wrong:

> in the 1950s, social workers and other professionals were preaching the virtues of domesticity to their female clients. The good mother, it was maintained, stayed at home and devoted herself full time to the tasks of

child rearing. Lower class mothers who were economically able to do so, were all too willing to follow such advice – only to be berated in the 1960s and 1970s by the same professionals who had now had their consciousness raised by the new feminist movement, for surrendering their autonomy as persons to the slavery of the household. (Berger and Berger, 1983, p. 48)

Recent right-wing critiques support this view. Those engaged in the debate about the underclass, for example, deplore the way in which middle-class values have been mocked and rejected as much by the institutions of the state as by those who constitute the underclass that is under so much attack (Murray, 1990; Green, 1992).

Critics of the bourgeois ideal would agree that the ethos of familism has been absorbed by the respectable working class but question, if this is so, who gains from it, especially since the ideal form of the nuclear family (father as breadwinner, domesticated wife as home-based service provider and diligent, obedient children) has rarely been the norm for large sections of the working class. Recent research (OPCS, 1993; Family Policy Studies Centre, 1994) has demonstrated just how varied household structure is in the present day, and there is no reason to suppose that variability has not been characteristic of household formations for at least several post-Industrial Revolution generations. How then do individuals reconcile the contradictions evident between life as they experience it and the ideals to which they subscribe? Even the Bergers recognize this contradiction when they acknowledge that it was only the 'economically able' lower-class women who could retreat to the home safe in the knowledge that they were living up to their socially approved ideals. The double shift (or Kollontai's triple burden) has long been the experience of women in industrial society. Barrett acknowledges this point and suggests, citing Bruegel (1978), that if anyone in the working class benefits, it must be men, but only in a partial sense, since acceptance of the familial ideal, by creating division of interests by gender, compromises class identity and solidarity. She concludes, however, that capital has benefited in two respects: by having at its disposal a cheap female labour supply and an industrial reserve army of women, and, in the shape of the household, a voracious unit of consumption.

Women's subordination

Feminists are mostly agreed in linking women's subordination today to the structure of the nuclear family and the ideology that underpins it, and identify the development of these and their hegemonic nature to the rise of capitalism. While this goes some way to providing an explanation of the contemporary position in structural and ideological terms, it does not account for women's subordination in other cultures, in relation to other modes of production.

There are two points to consider. First, implicit in the view that it is capitalism and the nuclear family that is the source of women's oppression is the possible assumption that women under other social formations were not 'structurally oppressed' (and yet few would argue that case). Second is the tendency to account too easily for women's acceptance of their subordinate role in terms, exclusively, of the hegemonic nature of the familial ideology, which, it is argued, captures the consciousness of both the bourgeoisie and the working class, both male and female alike. This may well be so insofar as it relates to contemporary Western society; it is difficult to point to any other major category of the population that has so systematically and so pervasively – and with so little trade off – been subordinated with so little resistance from within its own ranks. What other set of ideological attitudes has enjoyed such hegemony under capitalism? Working-class movements have periodically resisted appeals to the general or national interest that would in effect be oppressive to their own interests; members of racial minorities have failed to subscribe to the dominant class view of their inferiority. Feminism, by contrast, has had much greater difficulty in challenging women (quite apart from men) in their accepted view, which believes in the innate differences between men and women and which therefore validates their subordinate position.

However, very little attention is given to the apparently near-universal social forces that have generated gender divisions and, as a consequence, women's subordination, regardless of the structural form of the society in question. The reasons are perhaps twofold. First, in suggesting that women's subordination seems to be (almost) universal, there is a danger of falling back on to the biosocial reductionist explanation – that there are innate biological differences between men and women and that social arrangements that lead to fixed social roles for men and women are necessary preconditions for the continuance of the human race. Thus there is a kind of 'biosocial contract' whereby women reproduce and men protect and produce. Clearly, no feminist is going to accept that argument, but radical feminists go some way in that direction, although reversing the balance of power in the contract, with women having particular roles and also certain skills, talents and sensibilities as a consequence that are superior to those of men. Second, since women's subordination is so prevalent, it is difficult to do more than speculate about its origins – there are no contrary examples to investigate and test for similarities or differences, causes and effects. Also, speculation takes discussion too far away from any attempt at reasoned analysis. (There are, however, examples from the field of development studies that show the process whereby men are able to *take away* existing rights that women have, which might provide useful insights [Rogers, 1980].)

Nevertheless, it is reasonable to assert that in most societies – known either from historical sources or contemporary ethnographic accounts, or familiar to feminists as their own societies – women tend to have fewer rights than men and in general are subordinate to power that is vested in particular categories of men or in men as individuals. It does not seem to be a characteristic dependent on any mode of production or period in historical time. However, the *form* of that subordination will depend very much on the particular structural form of a given society in a given period. Perhaps the only conclusion that can be drawn is that its roots have something to do with the rendering of biological and social reproduction as 'domestic' and therefore outside the realm of public debate, hence the related invisibility of 'the domestic' in political discourse across cultures and centuries and the lack of any serious questioning of the denial of women's rights to equal status.

In modern Western society, it is clear that there are functional links (in terms of principles of operation) between the individualistic bourgeois nuclear family (either as a structure or as an ideological construct) and the consignment of women to the domestic domain, dependent on a division between reproduction, production and consumption. In other societies, it may be the descent and inheritance system functioning as a means of building alliances and negotiating political relationships, in which women are seen as objects with an exchange value and thus as expressions of male wealth and power: a division between males as actors and women as objects in exchange relations. Alternatively, gender divisions may be subsumed into a qualitatively different cleavage. Arendt refers to the divide between necessity and freedom, as manifested in Greek and Roman society. Thus women and slaves were part of that realm (the private), and relegation to this was regarded as a privation: 'a man who lived only a private life, who like the slave was not permitted to enter the public realm, or like the barbarian had chosen not to establish such a realm, was not fully human' (Arendt, 1959, p. 35).

For the Greeks and Romans, the business of *res publica* was all important; unless a man could participate in that part of social life, he was deprived of the central meaning of life. Women were simply ruled out of this. For the early Marx, gender division was based on private property – the division between owner and owned, which he referred to as the natural division of labour within the family 'where women and children are the slaves of the husband. This latent slavery in the family, though still very crude, is the first property' (Marx and Engels, 1974, p. 52). Engels revised this view later, subscribing to the Morganite thesis of an early mother-right overthrown later by patriarchy (under which the family conditions and gender divisions described by Marx then pertained).

In emphasizing the universality (or near-universality) of gender division, feminists are in danger of falling into the trap of claiming both cross-cultural universality of form and content and of ahistoricity. However, this is not so; they are able to demonstrate quite clearly the historical and ethnographic evidence that shows a wide diversity in form and content of gender division and that changes in manner and effect over time. Even within a single society at a given time, gender division has different effects for different categories of women. In capitalist society, which is broadly character-ized by the separation of domestic and productive labour and the existence of an exclusive, discrete domestic domain, women are variously located within the sphere of domestic labour. Some are able by virtue of class or status to delegate responsibility for the perfor-mance of domestic tasks to others (to servants, to younger female relatives, and so on). Other women are tied exclusively to it, while others may only be partially tied, taking on roles (at various levels and of various types) in the public sphere. While the role of woman as biological reproducer is predetermined, her role as social reproducer and the extent to which she is involved in production is to a certain degree less fixed (although broadly circumscribed by structural forces). However, it is the force of the ideology of familism, itself rooted in the individualistic principle, with its prescriptive assumptions about the 'natural' and 'right' position of women, that chiefly circumscribes and constrains the actions and thought of all women, regardless of the wide and often opposed differences between their particular class, ethnic or status positions.

It is in seeking to counteract the pervasive strength of the ideology that feminists have looked for alternative principles upon which to base their struggle. Since they identify the possessive individualism that provides the base upon which familial ideology is constructed as the fundamental source of their subordination, they have looked for oppositional principles upon which to base strategies of challenge. Since they locate the central problem of women's subordination in Western society as lying in the inner-directed, male-dominated nuclear family, with its clear, gendered separation of domestic and public domains (where the crossing of this separation creates ambiguous and conflictual situations), they have consequently emphasized collective alternatives to the servicing and socializing functions of the family, and an unambiguous opening up of the public sphere to women as well as men. It is these attempts and the philosophy that lies behind them that are considered in the following chapter.

3

Collectivism defined

Since the Enlightenment, political theorists of opposing traditions have counterposed individualism against collectivism and the value of freedom against that of egalitarianism. Individualists have argued that what they see as the most cherished human value – freedom – can only be secured and protected under a political system founded on individualism and an economic system based on the free-market principles of liberalism. Political and economic life under such conditions is to be governed by competition free from state interference; the role of government is to be reduced to a minimum; conduct is to be governed by a clear and limited body of law designed to protect the freedom of the individual.

As Duncan and Hobson argue, the rights of the individual are paramount:

> The indivdual has three great rights, which are sacred from arbitrary interference by the State. These are the right to life, the right to liberty and the right to property. They are indivisible. To allow a man [sic] to live, but to deny him his liberty, is to rob his life of meaning. To give him liberty, but expropriate his property, is to make his liberty meaningless.(Duncan and Hobson, 1995, p. 28)

Furthermore, for many who hold this view, any attempt to redistribute wealth on an egalitarian basis is not only wrong in principle, but also wrong in practice. The poor, whom such measures are expected to help, rarely improve their economic position; on the contrary, they lose many of the benefits that would otherwise be

47

available to them. Egalitarianism, the argument goes, leads to a decline in the will and ability to create wealth (Joseph, 1976) from which all might benefit, and the introduction of coercive policies by the state (necessary to achieve egalitarian measures) leads to a decline in the acceptance of the other functions – legitimate and minimalist – of the state as regulator of law and order (Friedman and Friedman, 1980). Furthermore, it is argued, in liberal, individualistic Western societies, the 'market mechanism... has created the increase of aggregate income which also has made it possible to provide outside the market for the support of those unable to earn enough' (Hayek, 1976, p. 139). It has been the 'ordinary person' who has benefited from Western capitalism (Friedman and Friedman, 1980).

The individualists have particular points of disputation with those of the collectivist and egalitarian tradition. In essence, though, their argument is that it is against human nature to seek to achieve equality by imposition. Joseph and Sumption sum it up in this way:

> To the extent that a sense of community is natural to men [sic] political intervention is unnecessary; to the extent that it is unnatural political intervention makes it impossible. Sooner or later every idealist whose egalitarianism is based on a belief in human brotherhood is bound to recognise that his quarrel is not with an economic system but with human nature itself. His quarrel is with the instincts of competitiveness and materialism, tempered by tenderness to individuals, the common denominator of every society which does not set out to crush the humanity of its members. (Joseph and Sumption, 1979, pp. 40–1)

Similarly, Duncan and Hobson (1995) believe that, contrary to the collectivist view of the operation of the market, human beings will arrive at 'altruistic self-interest', which will benefit others as well as the self, without any need for collectivist regulation. They attack the intrusive State because it denies individuals those authentic moral choices whereby the person weighs the consequences of his or her actions on the lives of others. Collectivists, they conclude, are 'repelled by the basic insight of the market economy: that the self-interest of one individual can further the welfare of others' (p. 291).

Collectivists, however, have a cogent and carefully argued response that both counters the claims made by the individualists against them *and* sets out their position in its own terms. It is this which will be explored in this chapter. First, we shall consider the defence of collectivism against its critics and then look at the various components of which it is composed. This will be followed by a review of how feminists over a century or more have incorporated it into their thinking.

The collectivist viewpoint

Collectivism's principled defence against individualism

Those who defend the collectivist viewpoint accept the importance placed by individualists on the value of freedom, but they augment the concept, suggesting that freedom does not stand as an isolated and absolute value. It depends rather on qualification: on one individual's freedom *not* impinging on the autonomy of other individuals; that the freedom of one individual must not be paid for by the denial of freedom to others; that freedom from certain evils is as necessary as freedom to do or to have certain goods.

Robert Blatchford, writing in the late nineteenth century, described society as a:

> union of people for mutual advantage. Every member of a society must give up some small fraction of his [sic] own will and advantage in return for the advantages he gains by association with his fellows. One of the advantages he derives from association with his fellows is protection from injury. The chief function of government – which is the executive power of society's will – is to protect the subject... the subject is to be protected by the Government from injury by his fellow-subjects. Here I traverse the position of the individualists. They will restrain the assassin and the passer of base coin, but they will not suffer any interference with the sacred liberty of the slum landlord or the sweater. And I fail to see their reason. (Quoted in Brown and Wright, 1995, p. 101)

Another nineteenth-century writer, T. H. Green, quoted in the same volume (p. 132), wrote in similar vein:

> We shall see that freedom of contract, freedom in all the forms of doing what one will with one's own, is valuable only as a means to an end. That end is what I call freedom in the positive sense: in other words, the

liberation of the powers of all men [sic] equally for contributions to a common good.

George and Wilding (1985), discussing the Fabian view of collectivism, describe two crucial attributes of freedom. First, belief in freedom implies a 'concern for equality... because if there are major inequalities of resources or of economic power, some men [sic] are in bondage to others'. Second, freedom is 'the product of government action rather than government inaction'. They quote Tawney (1964, p. 169) approvingly: 'the increase in freedom of ordinary men and women during the last two generations has taken place, not in spite of the action of governments, but because of it... The mother of liberty has, in fact, been law'.

Protagonists of collectivism would also take issue with the individualist belief as put forward by Joseph and Sumption (1979), that collectivist impulses are contrary to human nature and that there is something intrinsic in human nature that makes the values of competition and acquisitiveness more 'natural' than the collectivist values of sharing, altruism and cooperation. What Meacher calls 'fellowship' and others have called brotherhood (again both unfortunately gendered terms) represents as natural an impulse in human nature as the competition 'tempered by tenderness for individuals' does for individualists. Fellowship is placed 'at the top of the socialist value hierarchy' in Meacher's view (George and Wilding, 1985) and comprises 'the values of sharing, altruism and cooperation' (Meacher, 1982).

These values are at the root of the collectivist view of society, which sees them as those to which human nature, under the right circumstances, will naturally be drawn. It is a view that recognizes the primary importance of freedom (Hardy, 1981), but it is freedom qualified by the imperative that it must be accessible to all members of a given society – thus freedom for some at the expense of others is no freedom at all from the collectivist standpoint. The 'tenderness for *individuals*', which, according to the individualists, tempers the rampant and innate competitiveness of human nature, is in fact the charitable 'do-gooding' concern of the free and the powerful for those who are not free and who are powerless. It is the outcome of an inequitable and unbalanced power relationship. Collectivism, in contrast, starts off with a mutual, reciprocal and all-embracing concern for one's fellows as free, autonomous human beings –

Meacher's fellowship, Rousseau's fraternity and Marx's 'freedom in and through... association' (Marx and Engels, 1974).

Collectivism is both an abstract philosophical principle and a political ideology. It is frequently at this level that different approaches to the concept are manifested. In the political field, George and Wilding draw attention to three contrasting types of collectivism: first, that which they class as 'reluctant collectivist'; second, Fabian collectivism; and third, Marxist collectivism. Reluctant collectivists, they argue, will favour the adoption of collectivist measures *within* existing capitalist structures on strictly limited and pragmatic grounds, usually in the interests of efficiency and the need to regulate capitalism (which they do not believe to be capable of self-regulation). They tend to hold the same 'unproblematic' and unqualified view of the essential primacy of freedom as do the individualists. Fabian collectivists draw on humanitarian, altruistic and sometimes Christian traditions, seeing the need for an institutional and personal commitment to a social order based on those values which can be achieved on a reformist and gradualist basis over time. Marxists, in contrast, are sceptical of any truly collective arrangements even being possible within existing capitalist society. It is an article of Marxist orthodoxy that this is so. Any form of collective relationship under capitalism is a relationship warped by its class nature, since, according to Marx, such a collective relationship and the 'community' that ensued was always part of the 'combination of one class over against another [and as such] was not only a completely illusory community but a new fetter as well. In a real [that is, communist] community the individuals obtain their freedom in and through their association' (Marx and Engels, 1974, p. 83).

There is another type of collectivism in addition to the three described by George and Wilding, the anarchist conception of collectivism, which does not – contrary to the Fabian and Marxist viewpoints – see its achievement through government/state action. It is, in fact, a precisely opposite conception – the state is seen as an institution of bondage, and men and women can only be collectively free through free association unregulated by the state. As the Spanish section of the First International declared in 1872, anarchism would mean:

> the organisation of society in a vast federation of workers Collectives based on work, all authoritarian powers will disappear, converting themselves into simple administrators of the collective interests... Such

is the socialism that is proclaimed by the International of which the two
fundamental affirmations are: collectivism in economics and anarchy as
a political principle. (Leval, 1975, p. 24)

The goal was the same one that Saint-Simon had stated earlier
that century: 'to replace the government of men by the administration of things'.

However, political ideology has to be converted into practical
reality for ultimate goals to be achieved. The programmes for action
envisaged within the differing ideological traditions exhibit as wide a
range of variation as do the ideologies themselves. It is therefore
important to examine that variation.

The practical components of collectivism

The practical components of collectivism seem to fall into three
categories – one to do with *responsibility*, another to do with the
domain in which it operates, and the third to do with the *form* that
collectivism takes.

Responsibility   There are a number of levels at which collective responsibility operates. At its broadest, collectivism is about a
societal responsibility for all members of that society, a moral
responsibility that at the same time is translated into a practical
responsibility in relation to all citizens. The state may be seen as
steward of that responsibility, or, in the case of anarchism, all
members – the collectivity – are seen as bearing that responsibility.
At a narrower level, responsibility may be held by the local
community – the municipality, the neighbourhood, the commune
– or by a functional/interest group (women's organizations, trades
unions, professional groups, friendly societies, and so on). That
collective responsibility is concerned with ensuring the welfare of all
members of the collectivity or of particular specified categories
within it. Provision of care and support for those who are in any
way dependent is clearly part of that responsibility. Along with
responsibility for welfare is a responsibility for the production,
distribution and deployment of particular goods, resources and
services for the benefit of the collectivity as a whole or for certain
mutually agreed member groups.

The domain in which collective responsibility operates   Such a broad conception of responsibility clearly covers both the public and the private domains. Within the sphere of public affairs, collectivist principles are likely to be applied to a range of economic, political and social activities, such as industrial production, the public utilities, agriculture, the formal education system, the health care and welfare systems, and so on, but the principles of collectivism can equally be applied within the domestic domain. As soon as recognition is given to that possibility, the distinction between public and private begins to get blurred. In societies based on individualistic, familist ideologies, ideological *rhetoric* emphasizes the separation of public and private spheres of responsibility (however much in reality there might be interpenetration). Where social organization is structured on the principle of collective responsibility for the welfare of citizens in all aspects of their lives, no such rhetorical separation is made, and thus the burdens that go with that separation are alleviated. This is especially so in the fields of caring and the social reproduction of present and future members of the collectivity.

While socialists who do not share the feminist perspective are mostly concerned with the application of collectivist principles in the broader sphere of public affairs, feminists are especially concerned with their application to the domestic domain. In this way they seek to bring about a deconstruction of that domain and to dedomesticate the everyday business of caring and social reproduction. By breaking down the public/private barrier (which they regard as instrumental in their subordination), they seek to move forward in the struggle to challenge the gendered division of labour in all its forms.

Form   The different forms by which collectivist principles can be applied are numerous and relate both to political ideology and domain. At the level of macroeconomics, arguments have raged as to how best the productive and resource assets of a society might be collectively managed and stewarded. Lenin's democratic centralism, the 1945 Attlee Government's nationalization in Britain, Proudhon's 'mutuality', nineteenth-century French syndicalism and 1970s workers' control are all variations on the broad theme of collectivization at the macro level. At the small-scale level, and especially at the domestic level, the form in which collectivist principles might be applied tends to be more contentious. Many theorists and activists (mostly male it should be noted), whose macro level collectivist principles are impeccable, find it difficult to accept that the domestic domain might also be transformed. In writing about Spanish anarchism, for example, Richards (1975) stresses approvingly that its collectivist principles did not encompass the domestic domain, although the text that he introduces indicates that many of the Spanish collectives did indeed transform domestic arrangements, with collective childcare and collective responsibility for fair incomes within the household being assured.

Feminists, in contrast to their less perceptive brothers, see a need for the personal as well as the structural within the domestic domain to be transformed. If the collectivity provides collectivized forms of care, for example (for the sick and/or children), there has to be a willingness at the personal level to change what are often long-held traditional views on the appropriateness or not of such forms.

This takes us on to a later section of the chapter, which will be concerned with examining the ways in which feminist thinking about collectivism, as applied to the organization of daily living, have developed over the past century. First, however, we shall examine the notion of community as contrasted with that of collectivism, a notion that is often invoked as representing some of the same ideals as collectivism but which, it will be argued, represents almost the opposite.

Collectivism versus community

Since one of the purposes of this book is to take another look at the concept of 'community', as well as that of collectivism, this is an appropriate point to investigate further the meaning of 'community', which lies at the root of thinking on 'community care'. To the casual reader, it may seem that there is a degree of similarity between the two notions. Both, in some of their usages, conjure up pictures of warm humanity, altruistic concern for others and the cosiness of small-scale neighbourly relationships. Although left and right never unite in approval of the concept of collectivism – collectivism is seen as a partisan concept, as the 'emblem' of the left – it is remarkable how frequently both sides appeal to the spirit of 'community' to solve society's ills.

Notwithstanding the long debate in sociology since Tonnies (1955; *gemeinschaft/gesellschaft* conceptions of community) and Durkheim (1960; mechanical/organic social solidarity), and later Nisbet (1974; communities of interest characterized by social cohesion and moral commitment) and Bulmer (1987), there has been little attempt by those who currently use the term 'community' to define its meaning. It is thus not surprising that there is now a widespread consensus about those policies designated 'community care', since the idea of community upon which they are based means all things to all people. It has become a blanket term to cover all sorts of options. Those options may be composed of opposing orders, but the label is the same. On the one hand, there are those who advocate privatized options (especially for solving the problems of care); on the other are those who advocate socialized or collectivized options. Both call upon notions of community spirit to validate their views.

Those on the right see community as representing the sum of private individuals acting together in their own interests in opposition to the overarching state. This view is essentially a populist one: it counterposes the community of the 'little man', the powerless individual, against the monolith of the unfriendly and impersonal state. For the dependent members of society, community responsibility means *ad hoc,* informal, individually inspired responsibility. Primarily, supporters of this view stress the role of the family, proposing the family model of responsibility and care as the ideal, and at the same time extending the notion of responsibility to the community, defined as that grouping of families and friends within it. It involves a robust assertion of the principle of possessive individualism, reflected in statements made at the official level that expound the ideals of sturdy self-reliance, privacy and looking after one's own (Tebbit, 1986). Appeals to community responsibility in this sense do not involve notions of collective or communal responsibility – this would involve the surrendering of individual rights in the face of the state collectivity. Informal care networks, dependent on the presence of relatives and willing friends or neighbours, are expected to take on the bulk of responsibility for the care of dependent people. Voluntary effort of this sort is regarded positively; it is seen as a means of chipping away at the intrusion of the state that is manifested through the action of its agents, the professionals who provide the formal services.

Those on the left also call upon 'the community' to solve the problems of care and issues of responsibility, but from an opposing perspective. They see the community as the collectivity taking on responsibility for all its members, especially dependent members, regardless of family affiliations. In part, they recognize the same impersonality of the state as do those on the right, but they seek to personalize it rather than destroy it. Responsibility is to be collectivized or socialized rather than privatized. Some of the same worries are voiced about professional intrusion, but these are more to do with their lack of accountability to the collectivity. The state and its agents, according to this view, should be at the disposal of members of the collectivity – they have a better estimation of their own wants and needs. In addition, there is a conscious belief that private individuals should *not* be expected to take on what is thought rightly to be the responsibility of the collectivity.

In recent years, the struggle between left and right to co-opt the concept of community for themselves has become fiercer. The Conservative Party in Britain has talked about 'active citizenship' and the importance of local people being involved in community surveillance schemes ('neighbourhood watch'), of parents being involved in the management of schools and of the duties and obligations, rather than the rights, of citizens as members of the community. Those who adopt this position value the affiliations of nation, neighbourhood, pub, club, church and family as tempering the power of big government on the one hand and rampant individualism on the other (Willetts, 1992). In this way, it seems, the extreme free marketeers of the 1980s have begun to modify their position.

For their part, some of those on the left have become interested in a set of parallel ideas. They have become interested in what Amitai Etzioni calls 'communitarianism' (1995a, b). What at first sight seems to be a call to support collectivist ideals of social solidarity turns out on closer inspection to be an appeal to a narrow familist-dominated assertion of middle-class values, where control of dissident youth and single parents are regarded as first essentials. Tailored to meet the crisis of social fragmentation in American inner cities, communitarianism's concerns are understandable, but to regard it as an expression of older socialist, collectivist values is a mistake.

Community, then, is a term to be wary of since it lacks a coherent definition, at least in current usage. Under present conditions, it has been successfully co-opted by the dominant ideology and has become another facet of possessive individualism. In cases where the term is used to denote some sort of collectivist or socialized approach to issues of responsibility, it is better for the sake of clarity to stick with those terms themselves. The continued use of the word 'community' simply obfuscates matters.

The development of feminist approaches to collectivism in the organization of daily living

Collective or communal approaches to the business of daily living have been in currency in Western thought at least since the beginning of the nineteenth century. The French utopian socialist Fourier advocated communal forms of residence – *phalanstères* – and collective childcare. The 'home colonies' set up by Robert Owen were also ventures in collective and cooperative living. While Marx labelled the thinking of such people as Fourier, Saint-Simon and Owen as 'systematic pedantry' characterized by a 'fanatical and superstitious belief in the miraculous effects of their social science' (Marx and Engels, 1973, p. 61), it did give rise to ideas that feminists have since developed. Fourier and Owen were both concerned to establish new forms of living that would give women greater equality with men in relation to the domestic division of labour. Even Marx himself (in spite of his dismissal of the utopian socialists), along with Engels, envisaged a communist society in the future in which domestic labour would be undertaken communally, achieved by new developments in machine technology. Such emphasis on technological improvement was another occasion for disagreement with the utopians; Owen, for example, was keen to introduce intensive labouring methods such as spade-hoeing techniques into his communal experiments. Ruskin, some time after, had impossibly romantic ideas, seeing the future in terms of a 'back to nature' collective sharing of roles and duties based on the land and on crafts and manual labour.

Early feminist approaches to collective organization

It was during the latter half of the nineteenth century that the feminist movement developed, primarily around the struggle for the vote. On the whole, feminists were more concerned with achieving political rights than with alternative methods of organizing society, although the suffrage movement itself sprang from the broader socialist movement of the period. However, there were activists within it who were concerned with future demands and strategies (Garner, 1984). During the Edwardian period, Lady McLaren's Women's Charter of Rights and Liberties set out a comprehensive list of demands, amongst which were the requirements that:

Parliament shall compel municipalities to establish crèches and playrooms for the working class children, on the model of the German Pestalozzi Froebel House

Parliament shall compel municipalities in large towns to provide milk suitable for the food of infants and young children

Parliament shall compel municipalities to establish cheap eating houses and kitchens in working class centres on the model of those established in Berlin

Parliament shall compel municipalities to establish wash-houses appropriate to the needs of the community in working class or crowded localities.

While this smacks of middle-class maternalism, the key concept of the communal approach to the business of children's socialization and the hard tasks of domestic life is central.

Contemporary women critics of the suffragists, such as Dora Marsden, the editor of the *Freewoman*, who were highly critical of the reformist, non-feminist nature of the suffrage movement, developed a critique of the oppressive nature of women's maternal and domestic roles: 'group houses' with collective housework, or where professional domestic workers would be employed, were advocated. Marsden proposed state-run nurseries for children aged two weeks and older; woman's subjection to 'the three Fs' – food, furniture and floors – was abhorred.

Sylvia Pankhurst took these ideas beyond the level of mere discussion following her break with the suffrage movement led by her mother and sister. As a consequence of her disagreement with the Women's Political and Suffrage Union over their support of government war policy, she began to devote her commitment and energy to the support of working-class women in their struggle against the hardships caused by wartime conditions. Her East London Federation of Suffragettes set up a toy factory for women needing work, together with a crèche for their children. In addition, she set up a clinic providing medicines, clothes, baby care and information, along with milk centres and a cheap café. In her paper *The Women's Dreadnought*, she argued for 'free public nurseries' and communal restaurants. She stated: 'I believe in collectivism; in the collective action of free people agreeing on equal terms to subordinate the separate individual wishes for the benefit of the whole... the collective action of a free people for the common welfare'.

This was a view shared by the Russian socialist feminist revolutionary, Alexandra Kollontai, who argued similarly for collective approaches to domestic labour. In 1920, she argued that the advent of capitalism imposed a *triple* burden on women – childbearing and rearing, housework and then wage labour – that had become increasingly intolerable. The solution lay, she said, in words of 'this sacred motto: solidarity, comradeship, mutual aid, devotion to the collective life'. The communist society would provide 'public restaurants and central kitchens to which everybody may come to take their meals, central launderies and clothes mending shops', and also 'day nurseries, kindergartens, children's colonies and homes, infirmaries, health resorts for sick children, restaurants, free lunches at school, free distribution of text books, of warm clothing, of shoes to the pupils of educational establishments' (Kollontai, 1971).

During the same period, Dora Russell took up the theme of education as a means of creating greater collective care for all members of society. By providing education as a duty of the collectivity towards all children, it would be a 'sound preparation for really living democracy, instead of talking about it... [since] serious concern for children is likely to be implicit in a community that provides the greater part of their maintenance' (Russell, 1983, pp. 88–9).

Rowbotham suggests that the collectivist thread in feminist thought took a back seat during the 1930s, a development that was paralleled also in the Soviet Union. The attempts to put into practice there the ideas that Kollontai, Trotsky and others had written about were either overturned or put on ice; marriage and family life were re-emphasized. In Britain, according to Rowbotham, women activists in the labour movement were more concerned with abiding by the rules of the male institutions and strongholds, which they had finally managed to penetrate, than in replacing them with new forms of organizing and living:

> Feminism [in the thirties] meant more reforms, more welfare, equal pay. It did not mean any longer a rejection of a man-made way of seeing. It was no longer in opposition to the structure and culture of capitalist male-dominated society. The early vision may have been partial and

utopian, but it had been there. The feminists of the 1930s lost the earlier emphasis on sisterhood, on women doing things for themselves collectively, on the East London Federation's attempts to make a grass-roots organization. The feminists, like the Labour men and women, were let into parliament and put on committees. Once inside the constitution, they forgot that they had sought admission because they believed the world should be made anew. (Rowbotham, 1973, p. 162)

Thus the collectivist, communal ideal lay dormant. Feminism had become inseparable from the fortunes of the working class, since it was so closely bound up with the struggle for socialism, and as it went into decline, so too did the principles upon which it focused.

However, collectivist ideals did not die out completely. Jessie Bernard, for example, was discussing them in her study of American family behaviour in 1942, in which she emphasized the centrality of their place in socialist and feminist thought from Fourier onwards. They had been and still were the only solutions to the problems faced by women in modern society:

> throughout the 19th and 20th centuries socialists and feminists repeated essentially the same arguments as those he [Fourier] used. The spectacle of millions of separate heating systems, kitchens and laundries, of millions of women marketing individually and cooking individually and thus missing the advantages of a division of labor and specialization and machine technology, seemed to violate most of the canons of efficiency. (Bernard, 1971, p. 258)

Indeed, in the concrete world of policy implementation, the Second World War saw the practical application in Britain of aspects of the collectivist view, although brought about by the exigencies of war rather than from any acceptance of socialist or feminist principles. Women were drawn into the labour force to aid the war effort, and collective provision was made for childcare, although, as Lewis (1984) states, this was less available than is sometimes suggested. Many or most women still had to arrange childcare for themselves with family, neighbours or friends. Concern for the poor nutritional status of the population as a whole, and the need to distribute scarce food resources equitably (to prevent civil dissension), led to the establishment of a national food policy that involved rationing on a nutritionally sound basis and the development of people's restaurants, where the working population could be fed at minimum cost, with minimum disruption to working capacity. In addition, throughout the interwar and wartime period, the school meals movement had developed a momentum of its own; not only did it aim to satisfy the basic requirements of the children who ate them, but it also took on a messianic element, seeing the school meal as a means of socializing the children in citizenship as well as filling their stomachs (Le Gros Clarke, 1948).

These developments, then, can be seen in part as applications of the collectivist (if not the feminist) principle, whereby in this case the state took on responsibility for the care either of key groups needed at a time of crisis (the working population) or of groups whose welfare would be crucial for the future (in the health and welfare of children). Significantly, it was a form of care that had formerly been regarded as falling within the *domestic* sphere, for which the collectivity had no responsibility. Domestic arrangements such as these were normally held to be the responsibility of individual families, and of the women within them in particular.

Ironically, the Labour government elected in 1945 did not capitalize on these developments. While the new welfare state, built on the foundations of the Beveridge proposals, ameliorated conditions for broad categories of the population with its income maintenance schemes and free (at the point of use) medical care, it can hardly be said to have incorporated any of the specifically collectivist ideals of the earlier socialist and feminist movements. The domestic sphere was still essentially the private province of man the breadwinner, surrounded by his dependent wife and children. Where the public domain has subsequently intruded into this private province, it has largely been to police it. The development of large bodies of 'caring professionals' in the postwar period has had the effect of enabling the bourgeois state to maintain greater control over individual families, and to ensure 'proper' standards as embodied in the notion of the nuclear family (although Berger and Berger would argue the opposite).

Contemporary feminist approaches

In the immediate postwar period, with women returning to the home from war work in the factories and on the land, feminist thought continued to lie dormant – although this is a sweeping assertion, since it was during this period that de Beauvoir wrote her massive work, *The Second Sex*, first published in 1949, which feminists today regard as a milestone in the revival of the feminist movement. She was unsure, however, about how receptive women might be to her ideas and starts with a note of cautious misgiving, suggesting that perhaps enough had already been written on the subject and that perhaps the disputes of the past about the nature of the 'problem' were water under the bridge (de Beauvoir, 1972). Only in the 1960s did books and pamphlets begin to appear in any number, indicating a resurgence in women's consciousness of their subordinate position.

Their concerns initially mirrored the concerns of the time – personal liberty, freedom to express themselves, freedom for personal growth, 'getting out from under' the domination of men (and children). Gavron's (1966) study of housewives' isolation and frustration was an early example; Greer's *Female Eunuch* (1971) was largely concerned with exposing the sexual, cultural and psychological oppression wrought on women by men, as was Solanas's desperate credo of man hatred, the *SCUM Manifesto* (1971). At the same time, sober political analyses were developing, building on Mitchell's pioneering article in *New Left Review* (1966) and other well-remembered steps forward. A persistent theme of these was the need for a reorganization of the structures of daily living. The frustrations of the isolated housewife, as described by Gavron, were well recognized by the mass of middle-class women who were rapidly getting involved in the burgeoning women's liberation movement in the early 1970s.

One of the four demands emanating from the Oxford women's liberation conference in 1970 was the demand for twenty-four-hour nurseries, to allow women to be free from their children, in order to 'make the time to discover who stops us from living' (Wandor, 1972, p. 2). Thus childcare was seen early on as a major issue for the women's movement, both from the point of view of its limiting women's access to paid employment, and because the need to provide constant childcare impinged on women's personal freedom, on their own sense of personal space. Libertarian writers such as Greer advocated communal forms of lifestyle, since it maximized freedom for all those involved, adults and children alike: 'women must also reject their role as principal consumers in the capitalist state... they could form household cooperatives, sharing their work about and liberating each other for days on end' (Greer, 1971, p. 324). Political writers such as Rowbotham (1972) advocated the same because it represented a concrete commitment to the interests of women as a group rather than to the individual.

The theme was taken up widely by the movement as a whole. In the USA, Feeley expressed it thus:

> Socialists call for taking over the burdens that have been traditionally 'women's work' by socialising them. High quality child-care centres, staffed by people who enjoy being with children, would be a welcome replacement for the haphazard and almost non-existent care of today. Free communal dining areas serving attractive and nutritious food or prepared take-home meals would insure a better standard of health, and a well-paid house-keeping service, utilising scientific equipment, will help end the servitude of women. All of these services, controlled by those who use them, will free women from economic dependency on men and free children from the oppressed status within the home. (Feeley, 1972, p. 81)

In northern England, Comer (1973) echoed this view, expressing the disgust felt by many women in the movement at the individualization and consumerism to which they were condemned in modern society:

> The system demands that each family barricade itself in a small house or flat in order to fill it with consumer goods. We have only to look at a tower block of flats with 80 homes, each one of which will have its washing machine, Hoover, television, radio, iron, private kitchen with assorted gadgets etc. Now we have the technology to collectivise and eradicate most of the menial tasks which each woman in each flat performs in isolation from every other.

Political groups expressed the same views:

> We see the emancipation of women will take place when women are engaged in cooperative necessary work... much of (the housework) could be done away with. Restaurants, cafes, laundries, could be run as non-profit-making community services. (International Socialists, 1970)

and:

> We should be demanding an end to the privatisation of child care and housework. What we want is the socialisation of these tasks. (International Marxist Group, 1972)

The Nottingham Women's Liberation Theory Group wanted to augment the demands of the Working Women's Charter Campaign (strong in the mid-1970s in the trades union movement), to take account of these fundamental feminist demands:

> The Working Women's Charter is significant in this context since it attempts to deal with women's total situation in society although there is a danger that within the trade union context the demands affecting the personal and sexual freedom of women, e.g. abortion and contraception, nurseries etc. will be ignored. Bearing both these aspects of the question in mind we would also put forward further suggestions to fill out the Charter:
>
> 1. Community laundries and restaurants, etc., to free women from isolation in the home
> 2. Paternity leave
> 3. Shorter working week for both sexes to allow for a more equal responsibility for children and greater participation in all spheres of life. (Nottingham Women's Liberation Theory Group, 1974)

A decade later, Barrett and McIntosh (1982) also discussed at length the need for women to develop collectivist forms of living. They argued that the fostering of the 'domestic' ideal – focusing on the material enhancement of the home, with family members crowding in on each other within its narrow confines – cuts off many people who do not have such home bases from emotional solace. They also maintained that relationships within the domestic sphere are alienating and oppressive to those within, so that it has a doubly destructive effect, both to those whom it excludes and to those whom it embraces. They suggested that the 'iniquities of the family and its appeal are closely related – they are two sides of the same coin'. As an alternative, they argued the need to 'encourage variety, avoid oppressive relationships and beware of domesticity'. Communal living arrangements and collective childcare were seen as ways of doing this. They also recognized that one of the important caring functions fulfilled by the woman within the family is that of caring for the sick, disabled and elderly members, and they included this function too as one that should be socialized, along with childcare and housework.

Feminism's growing awareness of the issue of caring

The care of dependants other than children has become an issue in feminist thought only relatively recently. It is interesting to find that in the statements coming from the women's movement in the early 1970s, little mention was made of the family's role in caring for non-child dependants. In part it is a demonstration of the myopia and ego-centredness of the women who were becoming involved in the movement at the time. The previous decade had highlighted 'youth culture', and the emphasis had been on youth, freedom and self-expression. Young women's consciousness was being raised about their own personal situations – the claustrophobia of their marriages, the burden of isolated childcare and their resentment at losing the type of freedom that had been associated with their single status. Older women found it difficult to participate fully in the movement: if you were an ageing former suffragette, you were revered as an ancestress, but if you were merely middle-aged, there was little place for you. Thus the concerns of isolated middle-aged women caring for elderly relatives, nursing handicapped adult children or chronically invalided husbands did not figure in the consciousness of the women's movement at the time.

However, by the end of the 1970s, the caring functions of the family in relation to the sick and elderly had become a live political issue. Feminists may have become aware of it on two counts: either because they, as activists, had grown older and, from their own personal experience, had accordingly recognized new issues, or because in national politics the role of the family was being discussed and seen as a contentious issue. The decade saw an increasing pressure on the resources being made available to the health and personal social services, just at a time when demographic trends were leading to increasing numbers of chronically sick and elderly people in need of care. With the advent of the Conservative Government in Britain in 1979, discussion about the appropriate role of the family in relation to the provision of care and to the socialization of children and of the place of women in all this came to centre stage. Speeches made by government ministers at the time made it abundantly clear that the government regarded the family (and this was typified *par excellence* as the individualistic, bourgeois family depicted in the ideology of familism) as having a major role to play as a buttress against the intrusion of the state, as represented by its professionals, its institutional strategies and its income maintenance provision, into the domestic domain. The duties and responsibilities of families to care for their own members were stressed over and over again.

During the same period, academic analysis of social policy began to be penetrated by the feminist critique (Land, 1978). Increasingly, the debate in academic circles about issues of state and family responsibility for care, and the relationship of those issues to the health and personal social services systems, was being examined in terms of identifying the antiwoman assumptions underlying much of social policy, together with what the implication of this for women might be.

During the 1980s, more and more studies examining the nature of the domestic domain, relative to social policy and the role (newly recognized) of women and their families within it. They began to focus on the demands made on women by central government, which were seen to be closely allied to the development of community care policies. While some advocates of community care favoured it because it offered a less isolated and more integrated style of living to dependent people in need of care, the government began to emphasize that its support for such policies was closely allied to the view that families should take on responsibility for their own members. Fewer demands, the government argued, should be made on the resources of the state (that is, 'taxpayers' money'), and professionals should have less power to intrude into the private lives of citizens.

As a counter to this, a number of feminist studies were published demonstrating the effects of these policies and the assumptions that underlay them in relation to women. Finch and Groves (1980), for example, in an early paper entitled 'Community care – a case of equal opportunities for women', were perhaps the first to develop a feminist analysis of the issue, but it was only in passing that they referred to the possibility of developing improved forms of residential care as an alternative policy to community care. They were more concerned to emphasize the financial, emotional and career losses that women faced when they took on the caring role. Finch, however, developed the theme in a later paper:

> On balance it seems to me that the residential route *is* the only one which ultimately will offer us the way out of the impasse of caring: collective solutions would, after all, be very much in the spirit of a socialist policy programme and a recognition that caring is labour, and in a wage

economy should be paid as such, in principle should overcome some of the more offensive features of the various 'community' solutions. (Finch, 1984)

On the whole, feminists have been tentative in applying their principle of collective solutions to the care of chronically sick and elderly people, in spite of their readiness to see it as a solution to the organization of daily living for non-dependent categories (but including the care of children who, in the normal course of lifecycle events will remain dependent only for a *short* time), and perhaps with good reason, since Finch's article provoked a vigorous antifeminist response when it was published (Harris, 1985). While Finch was careful to emphasize that feminist-defined collective forms of care (both in terms of the group, be it the state, local state or neighbourhood, taking on responsibility *and* in terms of care-giving being provided in communally organized forms of living) would *not* mean a regression to the (still-existing) stigmatized, institutional forms derived from the later Poor Law period, the response has been both sceptical and hostile. The necessary hostility aroused by the worst examples of large-scale institutional care is too strong in many people's minds to allow for receptive thought about alternative, qualitatively different types of residential care.

However, while the collectivist approach has not been received enthusiastically in social policy approaches to the problems of dependency (Baldwin and Twigg, 1991), there have occasionally been signs that the broad principle of collectivism has found some favour in general political discourse on the left. Stedman Jones (1985) has emphasized the 'socialist commitment to the communal and the collective as a good in itself'. After all, he argues, 'socialism began life as a term counterposed to individualism'. He goes on to suggest that this principle has been reactivated in the socialist canon after years of barren and bureaucratic commitment to nationalization and 'statism'. Furthermore, this has been due *in part* to the influence of feminism since the late 1960s, when 'women attacked the patriarchalism of the nuclear family and the fixity of the sexual division of labour', thus contributing to the upsurge of creative thinking on the left in recent years. However, Stedman Jones wrote this before the later years of the Thatcher government, before the full development of community care policy, before the recession of the late 1980s and before further defeats of the left in the general elections of 1987 and 1992.

It remains to be seen whether a commitment to the communal and the collective will be able to offer a productive stimulus to new forms of social organization in both the domestic and the public spheres. Feminist concern with breaking down the conceptual barriers between 'public' and 'private' might unite with socialist ideals about creating 'a society in which forms of civic association and democratic participation are multiplied' as opposed to 'the incorporation of society within the state' (Stedman Jones, 1985). In the process, the welfare of those dependent for their care on public and private servicing might be enhanced.

4

Collective forms in the social organization of daily living

So far we have been concerned with the principles that have formed the basis of mainstream Western society – British society in particular – over recent centuries, together with the competing (collectivist) principles that revolutionary and reformist political activists have championed as alternatives. More specifically, the central issue of the book is concerned with how the application of those collectivist principles, themselves the basis of a complete sociopolitical philosophy, can be applied in the private domain in order to overcome the separation between the public and private domains that familist ideology seeks to maintain. A basis could thus be established for the wider application of collectivist principles, especially in relation to the provision of care for dependent members of society.

In this chapter, the discussion centres on actual examples of collectivist principles, past and present, as applied to the domestic domain. We shall discover how nearly they approach the aims and expectations of feminist thinking on the issue and how far they might be used as models for the future.

Such examples can be classified in a number of different ways: by origin (whether they have developed traditionally over time or were consciously created out of a hostile environment); by scope (whether they encompassed the whole of society or were retreats from wider society); by structure (whether they were organized on the basis of kinship or some other structural principle); by their underlying ideology (how far they were based on, or rejected, the patriarchal principle); by the implications that their particular forms had for women (whether women's solidarity was enhanced or fragmented). The list could go on.

What is significant about them all is the fact that they demonstrate, in all their diversity, the viability of the principle of collectivism. Even in Western societies governed by individualist principles – where the individualist mode has always been dominant, both in terms of intellectual debate *and* in terms of the assumptive worlds of 'ordinary people' – the will to develop communal forms, as Abrams points out, has never died (Abrams and McCulloch, 1976). It has repeatedly tried to reassert itself, especially in socialist and feminist thought. The histories of most Western nations show how often men and women have striven to put principles of solidarity and communality into practice, in opposition to contemporaneous modes of thought and practice. Many of those attempts, insofar as they have been 'holistic', have failed, that is to say, those which have tried to institute a completely new, integrated way of organizing daily life and work on a collective basis. The Owenite experimental villages, the Fourieriste *phalanstères* and the numerous nineteenth-century sectarian communities all foundered in due course, along with most of the 'alternative' communities of the 1960s and 70s. 'Partial' attempts at collective organization, mostly concerned with applying collectivist principles in the public domain, have had greater success. Organizations from within the working class have established themselves and flourished over time, founded on the basis of solidarity, mutual aid and collective action – trades unions, friendly societies, women's cooperative groups and the like, groups mostly concerned with solidarity in the workplace, financial insurance and social support.

Nevertheless, the individualist tradition is deeply embedded in Western society, and those who are placed within its culture find it difficult to comprehend alternative modes of thought. As the anthropologist Pitt-Rivers (1973, p. 90) says:

> A system of thought that takes the individual as its starting point and assumes that he [sic] is motivated by self-interest, faces a difficulty in confronting the example of behaviour that is not so motivated [but] the majority of the world's cultures do *not* share the individualism of the modern West and have no need to explain what appears to them evident: that the self is not the individual self alone, but includes, according to circumstances, those with whom the self is conceived as solidary.

However, Western individualists persist in regarding attempts at collective action (especially those which intrude into the hearth of individualism itself – the domestic sphere) as 'unnatural' and expect them to fail. Yet, as Pitt-Rivers states, the 'majority of the world's cultures' are based on a quite different set of principles and assumptions. Thus individualism is no more innate than is male chauvinism. Both are forms of learned attitudes and behaviour, framed by the ideologies and socioeconomic imperatives of particular conjunctures.

The role of kinship and its relationship to the subordination of women

Just as the nuclear, conjugal family upon which Western society is structured is based on the principle of kinship, so too, ironically, are most of the world's non-individualist cultures. Thus it is not kinship *qua* kinship that provides the rationale for individualist exclusivity (man the breadwinner, *his* wife, *his* children, *their* private domestic sphere exclusive to them alone). In many societies, kinship is the mechanism (or the metaphor) that provides the wider group with which the self can identify as solidary (in Pitt-Rivers' terms). It is the nuclear family, one kinship form among many, that has given kinship a bad name in the eyes of critics of familism. In other contexts, kinship provides the basis for collective action, collective support and collective identity. Fortes (1969) adopted the terms 'amity' and 'prescribed altruism' to characterize the nature and quality of collective kinship relationships; kin are required and expected to adopt these appropriate modes of mutual, reciprocal behaviour, thus providing the basis for the operation of collective relationships. In many societies structured on the principle of kinship,the principle can be extended beyond the strict boundaries of biological or affinal kinship. Non-kin may be classified as kin, and 'artificial' ties of kinship may be established, bringing into play the norms of amity and prescribed altruism, and allowing collective relationships to be extended beyond the biologically related group. Biological relatedness is not necessarily an exclusively defining characteristic. Amongst certain groups of Eskimo, for example, 'adopted' children become, in social terms, the true children of their adoptive parents, while grandparents may sometimes adopt the social status of parents towards their grandchildren (Saladin d'Anglure, 1967). This is not unknown on an informal basis in

Britain. Kinship or the metaphor of kinship, then, provides the basis in many societies for organizing widespread inclusive social relationships to mutual and collective advantage, just as it does in others for promoting small-scale introverted and exclusive relationships.

It would be foolish, however, to presume that all societies based on the inclusive principle of kinship operated to the advantage of the women within them, or at least not to their *dis*advantage, Likewise, it would be unwise to assume that *all* forms of living and working collectively, whether kin-based or not, were similarly beneficial to women. Greer (1985) has fallen into the trap of recognizing the theoretical advantages of collective forms but of failing to recognize the dangers insofar as they relate to women. She distinguishes between the family (nuclear, individualist and oppressive to women and children) and the Family (extended, members mutually supportive of each other, women non-dependent emotionally on men, appreciative of children). These are her definitions, and she suggests that the Family is fighting a last-ditch battle in the Western world (amongst Italian peasants, for example) against the encroachment of the nuclear form. While she may be correct in some aspects of her characterization of the respective family forms, she fails to acknowledge the specific nature of oppression as it resides in the extended Family form. The Family may well be appreciative of children, and in many respects it may well operate to its *collective* advantage, but Greer overlooks the narrow moral code that it imposes on women, the economic dependence of women on men and the domination of younger women by older women of senior status.

But what about *non*-kin-based collective forms? The evidence suggests that they may be just as likely to be oppressive to women. The studies of communes set up in Britain and the USA in the 1960s and 70s demonstrate quite clearly that the position of women was no more altered in the new forms of lifestyle than under the old forms (Rigby, 1974; Abrams and McCulloch, 1976). While men gained greater personal freedom, women were even more closely confined to domestic roles and subordinate positions. To make the issue even more complex, it becomes apparent, on the evidence reported from contemporary commune studies, that in spite of the formal structure of collective living upon which they were based, there remained an ideology of individualism running through many of them that was in stark contradiction to any sort of collectivist principle. Abrams, for example, saw them as attempts to embody the culture of possessive individualism free from the *contradictions* that individualist Western culture imposes:

> In modern market societies... such an ideal of self-property or self-possession becomes... the source of a cruel dilemma: humans can be human only to the extent that they possess themselves; but the conditions of the society in which they find themselves, and which establishes that very image of humanity deny the possibility of actual self-possession. [Communes therefore were attempts to] create pockets of freedom within such market societies, but sufficiently insulated from society for the ideal of possessive individualism to be realized without contradiction. (Abrams and McCulloch, 1976, pp. 189–90)

Thus the relationship between ideologies of individualism and collectivism and concrete forms of living and working is a complex issue. How far is it possible to examine the numerous possible forms of social arrangements that are encountered to identify both those aspects of them which are conducive to redressing the imbalance of women's subordination and those which actively entrench their disadvantaged position?

A typology of forms

By origin

Collective styles of organizing daily life can be defined in terms of their 'origins' or the tradition to which they belong. Thus some are those which have evolved 'naturally' or gradually through time, in the sense that they were not consciously constructed to develop particular collectivist strategies Our knowledge of them generally derives from ethnographies written by anthropologists. They are most likely to be kin-based. Others *are* consciously created attempts to develop communal forms but have varying conceptual bases. Some might be founded on religious principles, others on clear-cut political grounds. Some may be a mixture of the quasi-religious and the quasi-political, in the sense that they might be founded on a philosophy (however unarticulated) and have a political purpose (aiming to pose alternatives to current political structures). In general, kinship is less likely to be a criterion for membership but, because they are small-scale, links of kinship are likely to develop.

Examples from ethnography   It is clear from the wealth of anthropological literature available that there are manifold ways in which human beings have contrived to organize the daily business of living and working. One standard method of classifying this vast array is to look at degrees of complexity in forms of social organization, always with the caveat that it is important not to fall into the trap of social Darwinism, whereby it might appear that degrees of complexity might also imply some historically progressive development as well. The least complex form of social organization might be identified as the hunting/gathering group, as exemplified by the !Kung bushmen (Keesing, 1975). They are characterized by shifting patterns of residence, a simple gendered division of labour with little specialization beyond hunting and gathering and an elementary political system with leadership vested in a head but with most decision making taking place on a consensual basis. Bands of people ranging in number from twenty to sixty live and work in conjunction with each other. Links are informal and flexible: those born into a band retain their rights to live in its area and share its resources, even if they go to live elsewhere, and those marrying into the band gain similar rights. Lines recognized through both mother and father make for a closely knit mesh of kin relationships within the band, which commentators suggest enhances cooperation, unity and peaceful relations, both within the band and with other bands, since marriage links are made between bands as well as within them. While each band has a territory and has rights to the plant and water resources within it, outsiders may have access to water with permission, and band members may hunt freely in other bands' territories.

Cooperation and consensus are the keynotes in this clearest form of group living and working. Differences of a major sort are resolved by dissidents moving off and joining other bands or by forming a new one. This method of coping with conflict is clearly made more possible by the lack of political, economic and domestic complexity.

While a particular economic form demands collective, group action, it would be wrong to suggest that certain forms of living and working arrangements are merely responses to environmental imperatives. In the case of the !Kung hunters and gatherers, it could be argued that the social form most attuned to environmental demands would have been the strictly patriarchically defined band, with descent and authority reckoned in the male line only, and with women being exchanged out of the band on marriage and with strict territorial rights, instead of the rather fluid and consensual structures that exist in practice. Likewise, variation has been the keynote of more elaborate forms of economic organization, generating different forms of settlement patterns (New Guinea men's houses, Dayak long houses, West African village-based corporate kin groups), a host of different descent systems with related property rights (patrilineal, matrilineal, cognatic, and so on), and different forms of working patterns (working groups based on the nuclear family, the extended kin group, the village, the age set). However, characteristic of most precapitalist modes of production is the degree to which collective forms have provided the basis for living and working.

Thus in economies more complex than the simple hunting and gathering kind, where subsistence is based either on some form of agriculture or the domestication of animals, and where there may be some limited form of trade taking place, a variety of more elaborate forms of social organization invariably emerges to cope with the development of property relations, rights to land and other resources and rights over or in conjunction with other individuals or groups of individuals. Fixed residential settlements situated in close proximity to farmed land are typical of agricultural economies, and in pastoral economies, large mobile groups of herdsmen and their kin move together across the pastures. The division of labour is perhaps more complex: craftsmen and craftswomen may develop a sector of their own (leather, weaving or metalwork); agriculture and herding have their own techniques and skilled operators.

Living arrangements vary in these economies, but collective organization tends to be the norm. The independent, separate, elementary family seems to be rare in traditional societies. Stages in the developmental cycle of domestic groups mean that there are periods when the labour power contained within a single group is simply not sufficient to cope with the burden imposed by subsistence economies. The nuclear family, with several sub-adult children able to contribute to production alongside their economically active mother and father, has a different capacity from the same group a decade earlier, with a childbearing or nursing mother and several young children dependent for subsistence on the labour power of the father alone.

Collective arrangements vary. In some, the nuclear family may operate as a significant entity, cooperating with other similar units for specific (usually economic and ritual) tasks, but otherwise maintaining a separate existence. Alternatively, where polygamy is common, each wife and her dependent children may have separate living quarters and cook and feed separately from every other wife and her dependent children, but live within a common boundary such as a compound, cooperating with each other in the fields. Among the Tiv (Bohannon, 1954), for example, each woman would have a hut and a separate place to cook after the birth of her first child. As a woman increased in status – by numbering daughters-in-law or by being reckoned as senior wife – she would become head of a group of women and would thus be able to have her own granary. A compound might be composed of clusters of wives and their children, together with the wives of those male children and their children, placed in huts in careful relationship to their genealogical status within their lineage group (the particular form of kin group, based on a descent line through first-born males) and to the compound head, who would have a hut of his own. All those compound members, numbering up to forty individuals, initially divided according to the mother/children relationship, would co-operate as a unit in the production of food, the sale of cash crops, trading, weaving, and so on.

In other instances of compound living (see Smith, 1960), women do not separate themselves off from each other but frequently share the immediate domestic environment, cooking from one pot. Other communal arrangements are also similar – production and consumption relating to the domestic economy and distribution and exchange through the market all being organized collectively. Women might perform all manner of tasks together: cooking, serving food, threshing grain, gathering wood and water and harvesting ground-nuts, cowpeas and cotton. Men, too, might combine in work units for farming and building.

In most of these living and working arrangements, residential units are built up on a basis of kinship groupings, of which the fundamental unit is the mother with her children. Upon this foundation, other elements are incorporated – husbands (in patrilineal societies), brothers (in matrilineal societies), sons-in-law, daughters-in-law, grandchildren – or the basic units of mothers and children are linked together (as co-wives or sororal groups) and again consolidated by the linkages of husbands, brothers and other kin of different generations. Thus kinship is the predominant organizing principle upon which this collective 'building block' approach to corporate group formation is based.

There are other ways, however, of organizing working and living on a collective basis that certain societies have adopted, which do not necessarily rely on kinship as their main organizing principle (or as the metaphor by which social organization is expressed). The division by age and/or generation is one method characteristic of some East African societies, for example. Thus individuals are grouped together according to age and beyond that by generation (several age sets being incorporated into one generation set), and these form the basis for collective living, action and cooperation. They are especially characteristic of pastoral peoples, such as the Maasai and the Samburu (Beattie, 1964; Spencer, 1965), where the generation set of young men – the warriors – is the key group in maintaining the wealth and substance of the group (its herds) and in protecting it from the raiding parties of hostile groups. This generation set then moves up as it reaches a particular chronological stage from warriorhood to elderhood and takes on the collective political control of the whole group. Since women are excluded from these roles, they do not figure in this collective activity, but, according to some sources, they parallel these stages in their own forms of age differentiation.

Age and generation sets are not wholly confined to pastoral peoples – the Kikuyu, who are a settled, agricultural people, also have such a system. However, the nature of settled residence is different from the fluidity of pastoral life, and the fixed relationship to home and farmed land creates a certain tension, at least theoretically, between those ties to home and land and those to age set, which cuts across particular kinship relationships and territorial residence and property rights. In anthropological terms, it could be argued that this density and complexity of cross-cutting ties reinforces the sense of commitment and loyalty to the whole group of which a person is a part, while at the same time threatening that very commitment since various competing tensions are generated.

We have seen that kinship and age or generation are commonly encountered as principles of social organization, but there is a further one – gender. Most precapitalist modes of production exhibit a basic gender-based division of labour and social organization, at least in limited form and in conjunction with the other principles. A particularly clear and comprehensive form is found in parts of New Guinea, where boys and men live together in men's houses quite apart from women. In other societies, even where residence is not so segregated, tasks are strictly divided according to gender – men will perhaps herd and women garden, men will pot and women will weave. The division is never precisely the same across all societies, which refutes the oft-held assertion that there are certain naturally defined tasks for men, on the one hand, and women, on the other.

Finally, in this review of ethnographic examples, it is perhaps worth noting that, along with collective approaches to living and working, collective property rights, too, are an important factor. Rights to land and livestock are frequently vested in the group rather than the individual, and rights may be conditional rather than absolute, according to circumstances and need.

So far, then, traditional ways of organizing daily living and working on a collective basis have been examined, and evidence has been offered that demonstrates the widespread existence of forms that are quite different from those to which people in the West are accustomed. For those schooled and processed to believe that possessive individualism is a universal given, it is salutory to learn that other forms and ideologies have been equally as pervasive in other regions, in other epochs.

'Consciously created' communities   From time to time, the history of the ideology of possessive individualism has been interrupted by attempts to develop collectivist alternatives, both as retreats from the dominant ideology and as confrontational attempts to overthrow it, as embodied in the revolutionary socialist and anarchist movements. Those attempts which have been retreatist in nature, although numerous, have rarely been successful. This lack of success lies perhaps not in the inherent invalidity of their aims but because there can be no easy accommodation of possessive individualism, on the one hand, and collectivism, on the other, in a single society when the dominant ideology is so obsessively hostile to alternatives. When collectivists seek to retreat and isolate themselves from the rest of society, they seem to atrophy and die. Collective action has to take place within the mainstream of society in order to be fertile and bear fruit; it has to struggle continually for its existence *against* the mainstream ideology, actively contesting that ideology, rather than cutting itself off in the hope of survival.

The nineteenth century was a period rich in retreatist attempts both in Europe and the USA. Those in the USA have been described as falling into two categories – one based on religious and the other on politicoeconomic critiques of society (Kanter, 1972). They were often developed by groups who had fled from persecution or disillusion in the Old World. Those in Europe, too, represented a flight from what they saw as the ills of contemporary society. Kanter regards them as utopian experiments in 'voluntary value based, communal social orders'. They were characterized by a withdrawal from surrounding society, which they saw as evil or dangerous, in the sense that contact with it would be contaminating and lead to a weakening of their members' commitment and solidarity. Members of the Oneida community, for example, which was founded by a sect called the American Perfectionists, performed ritual cleansing after the settlement had been visited by people from the outside world. Whenever one of their members went into the outside world, she or he was subjected to mutual criticism sessions before and after the journey in order to be purified from outside contamination. The Shakers, another religious cult, founded in England but later fleeing to the USA, provided strict rules for regulating contact with the outside world. Individual contacts had to be reported, certain areas within the settlement were deemed off limits to outsiders and outside relatives were forbidden entry unless they were thought to be likely converts.

Those communities that were founded to pursue religious ideals (such as the Shakers, Oneida, Snowhill and others) based their adherence to the collective life on the search to be closer to God, away from the barriers and constraints imposed by surrounding society. In practical terms, the communities established by a wealth of different sects and cults developed a variety of different forms of organization. Some held all property jointly, including such things as clothing, while others retained varying degrees of personal property; some lived communally, with children being reared all together away from their parents, under the same roof. The Oneida community's 'Mansion House' was just such a place, where there were bedrooms, an eating hall, a library, recreation rooms, a visitors' room and a printing office. While the Perfectionists at Oneida practised 'complex marriage' – not monogamous marriage but highly regulated multiple relationships between group members – other groups such as the Shakers enforced rigid distinctions between the sexes and practised celibacy as far as they were able to enforce it. Shaker communities had separate households for men and women, with between two and six persons sharing sleeping rooms. The Zoar community also practised celibacy for a time and segregated the sexes, although less strictly than did the Shakers. Other communities, such as Harmony, allowed nuclear families within the wider group to live in households of their own, but emphasized other aspects of the collective life, such as communal working and ownership of property.

Of the communities organized on politicoeconomic grounds, most found their inspiration in the thinking of people such as Fourier, Owen and the anarchist Kropotkin. Owen himself was personally involved in the setting up of New Harmony in 1825, and his son Robert Dale Owen continued the involvement. Although New Harmony failed after a few years because of, it is said, lack of selectivity in the membership and the use of unsuitable buildings, it provided the stimulus for a number of further Owenite communities – Wanborough, Blue Spring and the Friendly Association for Mutual Interests at Kendal and Valley Forge, amongst others. Similarly, more than forty Fourieriste communities were established in the USA between 1840 and 1850, founded on the *phalanstère* movement started in France by Fourier but never successful there. Both Fourier and Owen had clear views about the need for collective forms of organization. Fourier envisaged his *phalanstère* as a community in a single building, while Owen saw his as a range of communal buildings facing on to a common square. In the Fourieriste community of the North American Phalanx in New Jersey, tasks were rotated wherever possible, and specialists were given no special, distinctive status.

During the same period, there were many similar experiments in Britain. Religion and political philosophy were again the motivating factors. Hardy (1979), for example, distinguishes four categories: the sectarian (religious-based, God-seeking), the agrarian socialist, the utopian socialist and the anarchist (both religious and communist). The rural–urban dichotomy, a product of the Industrial Revolution, was a motivating factor in the British context for the 'back to the rural idyll' yearning that underlay many of the agrarian socialist experiments. However, the Industrial Revolution and the advent of the injustices, exploitation and oppression that it brought for the working class also inspired the utopian socialist experiments of Owen and his followers, such as Mudie at Spa Fields and Craig at Ralahine in Ireland.

Commitment to the collective ideal was a feature common to most communities, but levels and degrees of that collective ideal varied from settlement to settlement. Ruskin's communities were based on an essentially romantic notion embodied in the Guild of St George, whereby the English countryside would be restored to loving, peaceful cultivation by English men and women for the common good. Land was to be worked communally, using the 'gifts of nature', without the aid of machinery; devotion to the aesthetic ideal would be promoted in all areas of life. Others were far more practical and were not much more than villages of like-minded individuals, with houses grouped together on the same land, either with or without collective rights to the land, but with very little other sharing or cooperation, particularly in the domestic context. The Chartist communities at O'Connorville, Lowlands and Sings End were examples – model cottages on individual smallholdings, situated on single estates. Each cottage had its own domestic rooms and outbuildings for stock, tools and equipment, so that family and working life were self-contained within the unit of the smallholding. The utopian socialist communities of people such as Owen were more systematically committed to the collective ideal. Owen developed elaborate plans for the collective life based in specially constructed communities (such as Harmony Hall), where the domestic tasks of childrearing, cooking and washing would be transferred to community responsibility. The New Forest Shakers, like their American counterparts, gave up all their material possessions to the community on entry, worked and lived communally (although segregated according to gender), even working collectively for outside farmers at harvest time for no payment, as a 'labour of love'.

The essence of the anarchist approach to collectivism was based on a view that power should be removed from the state and decentralized to a society reminiscent of the gilds, brotherhoods and village communities of the Middle Ages. Kropotkin, for example, emphasized integration rather than division, similar to Durkheim's mechanical/organic distinction and Tonnies' *gemeinschaft/gesellschaft* relationships. How the transition was to be accomplished remained problematic, and contrasting attitudes to the issue of violent transition was what distinguished communist and religious anarchism. The latter saw itself as based on the Tolstoyan view that it was:

> a revolutionary challenge, where the Christian foundations of life – equality, brotherly love, community of goods, non-resistance of evil by violence – would replace the principles that supported the family and the State as basic institutions of capitalist society. (Hardy, 1979, p. 174)

However, in practical, daily living terms, there was much that was similar between the two approaches. At Clousden Hill, one of the Kropotkin-influenced (that is, communistic) communities, money that the community earned or was given was pooled and each received pocket money; members ate communally and decisions were reached by consensus – even where votes were taken, the outvoted minority did not have to abide by the decision. Similarly, in the Tolstoyan communities, such as Whiteway, meals were prepared and eaten together, there was a communal laundry and land was held by the group. In fact, the deeds of the land were burnt to symbolize the commonality of property. There was complete sharing of possessions, even with outsiders.

While emphasis on the collective and the shared is basic to the theory of anarchism, there is, nevertheless, an internal tension within it. At the same time as emphasizing a need for integration rather than specialization and division, anarchist thought also stresses the value of the individual and that the essential requirement in any truly communist society is for the individual to be free. Communal organization is thus seen as the aggregation of separate individuals rather than as a merging and blurring of individuals into the collective whole.

It is this internal tension that characterized many of the communal experiments practised on both sides of the Atlantic in the 1960s and 70s. Participants in that movement saw communes as an opportunity to get away from the 'hassles of consumer society' to 'do their own thing', alongside others with the same views but not with any intention of suppressing or transmuting their egocentricity. Those communes documented by Abrams and McCulloch (1976) and Rigby (1974), were set up with clearly articulated intentions to pool reserves and share domestic tasks and (sometimes) productive labour, but frequently fell apart because of individuals' dissatisfaction with the burdens of collective living.

They thus possessed the ingredients of failure in common with many of the nineteenth-century communities. That failure perhaps can be accounted for in a number of different ways. It may have been that the internal tensions between individualism and collectivism proved too much, it may have been due to their being deliberately cut off from mainstream society, or indeed they may have failed precisely because they were *consciously created* as separatist enterprises unrelated to the socioeconomic environment around them.

There is one example, however, that proves that not all such enterprises have failed: the kibbutz movement that developed in Palestine before the Second World War. Many have argued that its success has been based on the fact that, although it was consciously constructed, it was firmly rooted in the ideological aspirations of the new and growing Jewish society. Even so, commentators of various and contrasting persuasions have argued that kibbutzim are not completely successful in terms of their original aims and are moving away from the collectivist ideal. Irvine (1980), for example, has suggested approvingly that this is so because members have become more familist in their outlook (and, by implication, this is because it is a natural way to feel). Rodinson (1973), taking a political view, suggests that there is an inherent contradiction between the socialist, collectivist ideals of kibbutz culture and the essentially colonialist and racist exploitation of the surrounding Arab population, upon which wider Israeli society is based, and that this has diverted the movement from its original ideals.

Indeed, Buch, (1973) denies that those original ideals ever really existed; the movement has been 'far more important for settling new territory and guarding borders against dispossessed Arabs than for opening up a road to Jewish socialism'. He further argues that kibbutzim are part of the utopian socialist tradition, inevitably doomed to failure, and not the outcome of a social revolution – the only reason why they could possibly succeed according to his strictly Marxian scientific principles. Contrary views, however, have been expressed. Kanter (1972) cites Menachim Rosner, who argues that kibbutzim have been successful precisely because they have not been utopian socialist experiments isolated from the mainstream of society; Buber, too, according to Kanter, regarded the kibbutz movement as 'an experiment that did not fail'. Clearly these writers were able to consider the kibbutz movement as an exemplary and successful socialist experiment planted firmly within the framework of the ideology and structure of Jewish society and did not feel it necessary to address the issue of the unequal relationship between Jews and Arabs.

Even a brief glance at some ethnographic and historical evidence shows that the principle of collectivism has occupied a central place in the conceptual and structural systems of many diverse peoples. There are numerous non-Western societies where collective forms have developed and persisted through time as the dominant mode of social and economic organization. Because they tend to be small scale in size and organization, kinship has generally been the chief principle upon which collective life is based, although in such kin-based societies, other principles, such as gender or generation, may also operate to pursue the collective form. Even in societies (notably Western societies) that are characterized by an ideology of possessive individualism and where social organization is highly fragmented with a highly specialized division of labour, there have always been attempts to pursue the collective ideal. There has always been a belief that collective forms can transcend the alienation and isolation that are seen as the reverse side of individualism and that shared activity in production, social reproduction and consumption offers more humane alternatives.

Strength of patriarchy

Such collective forms may not offer these humane alternatives to all the actors involved. It may be that there are differential benefits, hence the second major category of the threefold classification of collective types: the manner in which collective forms can be classified according to the strength of patriarchy exhibited in both form and ideology. Patriarchy is defined here as structured and ideational male dominance, not specific to any one particular mode of production and not referring specifically to rights vested in the father as some would argue, since there is a wealth of anthropological literature showing that brothers are as instrumental in the subordination of woman as are fathers. Barrett (1980) has discussed the problems of defining patriarchy, suggesting that it is valid to use the term as descriptive of ideology but not as an entity in itself. Even so, she restricts it to ideological aspects of male–female relations within capitalism.

In examining a range of societies with differing forms of socio-economic organization, I shall use the term patriarchy, in spite of Barrett's strictures, to denote that mechanism whereby, in a given society, men are in general able to dominate women, a mechanism that reinforces social structure, which in turn then nourishes the ideology of patriarchy. Thus the degree to which men dominate women varies according to the society in question, depending on a number of factors, of which mode of production may be one and the descent system another. Therefore, urban Muslim women who are excluded from public affairs and physically consigned to restricted areas of the domestic environment suffer more acutely from one particular expression of patriarchy than do, for example, West African women market traders. In that part of Africa, there is a tradition of market trading in which women wield considerable economic power in the public sphere and have a freedom of action both publicly and privately that women in other societies would hardly recognize. Elsewhere there may be a public rhetoric of equality between men and women, but examination of how things work out in practice may reveal a different balance in the relationships of power between the two. Conversely, there may be a dominant view of women's subordinate position, yet in practice they may wield considerable power.

It is often difficult to elicit information on this issue from ethnographic evidence, since the anthropologists who collected the data have rarely been concerned with assessing any implications there might have been for women of a particular descent system or division of labour. This was particularly characteristic of those investigators who viewed 'primitive societies' as cohesive, harmonious wholes (under the influence of the Radcliffe-Brownian school of structural functionalism), where social institutions were seen to be integrated or finely balanced against each other, each having its part to play in the maintenance of the social system. It was difficult for them to see in the systems they were describing, where women might form a medium of exchange in the welding of relationships between groups, that the women concerned might have been having a raw deal. Similarly, the historical evidence is also open to the bias or value judgement of both the historian and the original source. The historian may see the position of women as being of little analytical significance and thus fail to present relevant data, while the values and assumptions of the original source may distort the evidence. William Morris, as quoted by Coote (1985), provides a good example of such value judgement. He obviously saw no need to question the old values about woman's place, when contemplating a classless society beyond class tyranny that they, as socialists, were struggling to achieve, for 'women do what they best can do... it is a great pleasure to a clever woman to manage a house skilfully... and then, you know, everybody likes to be ordered about by a pretty woman'. His view of gender equality was unlikely to have borne any relationship to the views of contemporary feminists.

There is some evidence, however, that gives an indication of how women have fared in these collective settings. In most of the ethnographic evidence, patriarchal forms predominate. In patrilineal societies, for example, where descent and inheritance are reckoned in the male line, women marry out of the patrilineal group into other men's patrilines. 'Strength' of patrilineality might vary – in some cases patrilineal groups may retain rights in their women who marry out, in other cases the patriline into which the woman marries may take over all rights in her, severing the rights of her own patrilineal group. Whichever group obtains or retains the rights, it is certain that the woman herself does not hold them. Thus the power and solidarity of the collectivity is predominantly a male construct. Women within patrilineal societies may cooperate on a daily basis in the business of production and social reproduction, but it is men who comprise the corporate political and economic identity of the group that can correctly be described as patriarchal.

Even in matrilineal societies where descent and inheritance are reckoned in the female line, men still retain rights in women, the men in question being brothers rather than fathers. While it is fathers in patrilineal societies who forge the marriage alliances between their daughters and other men's patrilineages, in matrilineal societies it is a woman's brothers who have the right to do this for her daughters. Perhaps a major difference is that in such circumstances it is the new husbands who are in the ambiguous position: they may or may not move to live with their wives on marriage, but they are also brothers with rights in their sisters' daughters, which they pass on to their sisters' sons. The sororal group of women with their children, brothers and uncles, and with their husbands relating to them on the periphery of this nucleus, offers more possibility of collective, solidary support than is available to those women in patrilineal societies, taken from their natal group at marriage to be lodged, physically, in the bosom of an often unknown group, dependent on the uncertain reception of the new group's womenfolk. Kinship here offers security to those who are born into the group but may also act as an excluding mechanism to newcomers, who then have to spend many years learning to fit into and be accepted by their new (affinal) kin group.

Few traditional societies seem to articulate any notion of gender equality, but some may display a less rigid gendered division of labour than others, and this is sometimes associated with a general lack of complexity in social and economic organization as a whole. A more rigid division is often, but not exclusively, associated with an elaborate and specialized division of labour – some urban Muslim societies show these characteristics, societies that are also characterized by a well-articulated religious ideology that promulgates a particular view of women and their 'rightful' place in society. This acutely gendered division of society is familiar, too, in those 'residually traditional' areas of Western society, such as the Italian villages described by Greer (1985). Here the social organization of domestic life is still based on kinship – the Family, in Greer's terms – and women occupy specific and restricted spheres separate from the male world of public business. The residually traditional areas of Mediterranean society as a whole are characterized by this system, the institutions of 'honour and shame' acting as regulatory mechanisms to ensure that women do not step outside their prescribed social territory (where they have degrees of power and influence). If they do so, it would bring shame and dishonour upon their male kin (Peristiany, 1974).

By and large, then, it seems that while the majority of kin-based societies have well-developed collective structures, they tend to have an underlying patriarchal ideology that roots women firmly in a disadvantaged position *vis-à-vis* their menfolk. In the business of daily living, collective forms may make their tasks less irksome and isolated, but in political, economic and legal terms, women do not fare well. As regards patriarchal ideology, there is perhaps little difference between such societies and Western capitalist society where, it has been demonstrated earlier, gender inequality is similarly entrenched. At the level of public discourse, however, there may be some difference: in Western society, it is frequently asserted that there is no inequality, while in traditional society the issue simply may not be addressed, or at least not seen as problematic.

Where, then, are there any examples of societies in which there is conscious ideological commitment to gender equality and a denial of patriarchy? Evidently some of those communities that were set up to develop the collectivist principle aimed also to redress the balance of inequality between the sexes, but they were established within but separate from a patriarchal, individualist host society that was bound to exert its own influence and pressures on the new experiments. Even where there was commitment to overthrowing patriarchal forms, it is unlikely they would remain uncontaminated by the influence of the surrounding order or the implicit assumptions that members brought with them from the past. The utopian socialist communities based on the thinking of both Fourier and Owen, for example, consciously sought to release women from their traditional roles. There were various strategies, ranging from the collectivization of domestic tasks – in which men were also to participate – and communal childcare, to simple forms of dress and personal adornment. In practice, however, role specialization often persisted in an unquestioned way. The Co-operative and Economical Society, which set up a community at Spa Fields in London in 1821, is a case in point. Their domestic practices were described in *The Economist* in 1822:

> The domestic duties of the females are performed under a system of combination, which greatly lessens the labour and enables females either to be profitably employed or to command a considerable portion of leisure for rational pursuits and innocent recreations... such of the females as are not required for the discharge of the duties of housewifery and for the care of children, are employed during a moderate portion of the day in such profitable work as can be obtained for the benefit of the society at large. (Hardy, 1979, p. 45)

In many of the religious or sectarian communities that were set up, gender equality was furthest from their thinking; many of their ideas revolved round the need for celibacy and sexual segregation. The Shakers, for instance, while living communally, rigidly separated men and women, regulating all contact and replenishing their numbers not by biological reproduction but by the recruitment of outsiders. Of course, sexual segregation does not necessarily mean that women in the new communities occupied a subordinate position, but anthropological evidence suggests that where women are strictly segregated from men, there are frequently accompanying beliefs about the ritual dangerousness of women and their polluting characteristics, which lead very quickly to their devaluation as a category. In the context of the new communities, sexual segregation and free love were the two sides of a single problem in communal living – how best to regulate intragroup male/female relationships while preventing the development of 'couple' relationships, which, it was felt, would threaten communal commitment. In both sorts of community – those practising celibacy and those practising free love (celibate Harmony in the USA during the nineteenth century and

the many modern free love 'hippy' communes in the 1960s and 70s)
– there is evidence to show that women's subordinate position
remained unaltered. It is difficult to demonstrate evidence of gender
equality being achieved in either sort of community.

There were conscious efforts at overthrowing patriarchal forms in
some of the anarchist experimental communities of the late
nineteenth century. The community at Whiteway is an example,
where women did the same work as men, yet men failed to participate in domestic tasks (another example of the woman's double
burden). Even in kibbutzim, where the collectivist principle has been
most nearly put into practice, it is recognized that women have been
excluded from playing a full part in the public sphere of kibbutz
economic and political life, being restricted to less significant sectors
(in which the caring and servicing functions have been central).

So, in examining the record of experiments in communal living,
it appears that the pattern of women's subordination and restriction
is repeated again and again, even where there have been explicit
attempts to revalue their position and construct equal access to all
sectors of the life of the community. The reasons may be those
which are considered to have been instrumental in the failure of the
communities themselves – the impossibility of setting up communities within, but apart from, an oppressive mainstream society.
Communitarians might argue that, by example, they act as catalysts
for change within society as a whole; critics would argue that
without a thorough-going social and economic revolution, change
of such a fundamental nature – both at the ideological and
structural levels – will never happen. Perhaps most significantly of
all from the modern feminist viewpoint, there has never been a
sufficiently analysed and theorized exposition of women's oppression incorporated into collectivist theory and ideology, in whatever
time or place.

The solidarity of women

This takes us to the third of the threefold classification of collectivist
types – the manner in which a particular form affects women, the
consequences for women. Inequality and subordination can have
two outcomes: those subordinated may perceive their state of
inequality and dissent either openly in active resistance or in passive
non-cooperation. On the other hand, they may fail to recognize their

oppressed position, accepting it perhaps as different from their masters – different yet equal. Having internalized the values of those who dominate, their own status becomes unremarkable. They may even recognize their inequality but accept it as just, according to the tenets of an explicit ideology.

In societies where living and working may be collectively organized, women may develop high degrees of solidarity amongst themselves, perhaps in opposition to high levels of male dominance. However, social organization may militate against women's coming together in mutual support and identification, in spite of the collective forms that bind their menfolk together. In an introduction to a collection of papers concerned with examining the nature of women's solidarity, Bujra (1978) seems to limit its definition to solidarity conceived of in a Marxist sense – a solidarity borne of collective consciousness (feminist as much as class) and hence potentially subversive and revolutionary. She tends to discount those forms of women's unity which are partial or partisan, in the sense that they relate only to fractions of women within a total society. Thus she suggests that the identity of interest that middle-class women on an English housing estate exhibit, as described by Cohen (1978), actually reinforces the class privilege deriving from their husbands' 'objective positions in the class hierarchy'. Even in contexts where there are collective forms (which is not the case in Cohen's study), women's unity of action or interest may not transcend other structural divisions. Bujra is clearly suggesting that whether or not women can 'truly' join together in solidarity depends on their position in the relations of production. Thus only if women occupy a single (and exploited) position (as does the working class) can they have an identity of interest and the ability to join in conscious solidarity against dominant interests.

This is a perfectly legitimate approach, but it tends to obscure differences in 'non-conscious' forms of solidarity, which may be of analytical importance, especially in trying to come to an understanding of the nature of male dominance and its consequences (not just in capitalist relations of production). Since the collective organization of daily work and living is proffered by feminists as a means of raising women's subordinate position, it is important to try to identify those instances where this does not happen, in spite of some degree of collective organization, in order to aid the search for explanations of why it does not.

But how do women actually behave in these circumstances of subordination? Different patriarchal forms generate different responses. Women may, in certain circumstances, form close relationships with each other and live a collective life, supporting and tending each other and deriving mutual satisfaction from this solidary organization. In other circumstances, the features of their oppression act to fragment women and separate them from each other, so that the compensating effect of solidarity in the face of extreme oppositional forces is missing. Only rarely do women collectively perceive the reality of their oppression, and even more rarely do they act collectively against it. More often than not, according to the ethnographic evidence, this collective action tends to be symbolic and thus incorporated into the ritual life of the society, rather than threatening the fabric of its social structure.

The pattern of these responses is unclear; in contexts where women suffer extreme subordination and/or segregation, there are situations where the 'solidary' response in terms of mutual aid and support is highly developed. Women in Muslim Morocco are restricted to a physically defined female sphere and develop their own collective, emotionally supportive networks (Maher, 1976). On the other hand, women in Hindu families in rural India, who are similarly subordinated, occupy an explicitly but informally segregated position but tend not to develop such supportive networks because they are subject to a clear authority structure based on women. Thus young stranger women marrying into the family will become subject to the authority of senior women – the mothers and aunts of their menfolk – which militates against the development of mutually supportive networks (Sharma, 1978). However, Melissa Llewelyn-Davies (1978) describes processes of female solidarity operating in Maasai society even though stranger women marrying into the group initially have to break through explicit and sometimes violent hostility on entering it.

Women in these societies are similar in the extent to which they lack autonomous economic power. In other cases, where they do clearly have some economic autonomy, they are also shown to have developed solidary networks. Nelson describes the manner in which daily cooperation amongst Nairobi women in the production and sale of maize beer supports a wider solidarity amongst the same women (Nelson, 1978). In that case, it is unclear how far economic cooperation is the predetermining factor for the emergence of such networks and how far the hostility of surrounding society is more significant (since women from Mathere are regarded as prostitutes, outside the norms of 'respectable' society). The supportive networks developed amongst West African market women, who have a great deal of economic power and occupy less marginalized positions *vis-à-vis* mainstream society compared with the beer producers of Nairobi, are similar examples, although in less ambiguous situations.

Thus, while many societies exhibit collective forms in some aspects of their socioeconomic organization, these do not necessarily contribute towards the development of gender equality or of female solidarity. Degrees of patriarchy, levels of women's subordination and the extent of female solidarity all seem to exist independently of the degree to which the principles of collectivism are present in a given society. *Unless there is an explicit ideology of gender equality*, egalitarian and collectivist principles only seem to operate fully in relation to men. In the context of this inequality, women adopt varying strategies of 'getting by', in some cases by developing mutually supportive networks, in others by participating actively in fragmenting and isolating strategies in which some women will achieve power (within the domestic context) and others will be dominated both by men and by senior women.

Yet, in societies in which there might be some public declaration of gender equality but in which there is little evidence of any adherence to egalitarian and collectivist principles in general, women still seem to be relegated to a subordinate role, as is the case in contemporary Western society, where there is frequently a statutory commitment to gender equality but in practice a conventional exclusion (Sharma, 1978) of women. Clearly public declarations of commitment to gender equality are insufficient. At an ideological level (in terms of internalized values and assumptions), there remains no such commitment; this seems to be so as much in the case of alternative experimental communities in Western society as in the case of mainstream society. Those nineteenth-century communities described earlier as having some commitment to redressing the balance between men and women and those more recent hippy communes referred to earlier all failed to do anything about it in practice. Solanas's (1971, p. 13) bitter description of the 1960s failure to do so is a pertinent comment:

The 'hippie', whose desire to be a 'Man', a 'rugged individualist', isn't quite as strong as the average man's, and who, in addition, is excited by the thought of having lots of women accessible to him, rebels against the harshness of a breadwinner's life and the monotony of one woman. In the name of sharing and co-operation he forms the commune or tribe, which, for all its togetherness and partly because of it (the commune, being an extended family, is an extended violation of the females' rights, privacy and sanity) is no more a community than normal 'society'.

Collectivism and a commitment to the collectivist ideal, then, is a complex issue when applied to those functions normally associated with the domestic domain. (It is apparently a lot less problematic for socialists – especially male ones – to apply the concept to the public sphere, in their appeals to working-class brotherhood through trades union solidarity and action.) Those numerous societies that have traditionally been based on collectivist principles have, in the main, been structured on highly developed forms of patriarchy. Women fare variably within them. Within confined limits, they may benefit at a practical level, sharing tasks cooperatively but within a special-ized and gendered division of labour. They often develop particular forms of female solidarity to support each other, which may sometimes be symbolic (and ritualized in certain circumstances) of the latent opposition between men and women; on the other hand, women may be opposed to each other and show little evidence of mutual support. Economic and political power is usually denied them. Where women do unusually have economic power, there is evidence of supportive networks underpinning it – and such power is of crucial significance.

Where there have been experimental attempts to set up collec-tively-based communities, they have rarely been successful, and women have, again, been unable to establish themselves on an egalitarian basis with men. Failure of these attempts is generally accounted for in terms of their isolation from mainstream society and their lack of grounding in the structural forces surrounding them. Although in real terms such communities may not have been significant, as *concepts* they represent part of a continuing critique of the dominant ideology. While some were established purposefully to pursue strategies of gender equality, it seems that prior values are hard to get rid of, and the old attitudes have been carried into new contexts regardless of professed aims and objectives.

There are perhaps three profound lessons to learn. First, collectivist principles can be found working successfully, but they cannot be applied in isolation from mainstream society. If this is so, they must be applied from within, as a direct challenge to the structures and institutions that surround them. Second, collectivist principles in themselves do not necessarily carry with them notions of gender equality. Such a notion must be linked explicitly to the collectivist form for it, or for both, to have any chance of ever being accomplished. Finally, a highly developed analysis and theory of women's oppression that builds on that recognition of gender inequality has to be incorporated into any programme of theory and action.

5

Collective responsibility for dependent people

In the previous chapter, we looked at the collectivism that underlies the social organization of daily living but did not consider how those societies and communities attempted to provide care for their dependent members and whether or not they were based on a collectivist approach. This forms the central focus of the present chapter, and a similar mix of ethnographic and historical evidence will be used to consider how (or whether) underlying ideologies of collective responsibility have been brought to bear on the tasks and forms of caring.

Clearly the organization of caring in a given society is closely linked to the way in which that society organizes other aspects of social relations. The same values and attitudes come into play. Thus in modern Western society, it is attitudes towards the nuclear family, encapsulated in the ideology of familism, that are the key to patterns of care. Within the context of the family, under normal circumstances, responsibility for fulfilling the caring, nurturing function in relation to the rearing of children and the servicing of adult family members falls upon the woman. Likewise, by extension, women within the family are expected in 'extranormal' circumstances to care for the chronically dependent (physically and mentally disabled adults and children, frail and confused elderly people). Where society takes on responsibility for providing care, the form of care adopted has tended to be modelled closely on the familial model. The postwar period has seen a consolidation of the guiding objectives underlying formal care policies, promoting dependence on the familial model of care above all others.

It is ironic that official discourse should have proclaimed the family as the ideal model on which its social care should be based just at the time when the family, with all its ramifications, was coming under mounting criticism from feminists and, to a lesser extent, the 'anti'-psychiatrists (Cooper, 1971) and the left. It was suggested earlier that contemporary official policies are based on an individualist approach to welfare, placing value on self-reliance, independence and minimal state provision, where families can take on most of the burden. In addition, they are policies that are essentially anti-collectivist. In contradistinction to its founding principles, the welfare state as steward of collective responsibility is increasingly expected to adopt a residualist role, supporting private effort rather than taking a lead; along with this, collectivist *forms* of care have come to be seen as inappropriate. The family therefore becomes central; collective responsibility, as it resides in the state, becomes merely a back-up to private provision. In the 1990s, nowhere is this more dramatically seen than in the case of long-term care for older people. More and more of them are being moved into private residential or nursing home care, for which they or their families have to pay, despite policy objectives that state that they should be maintained at home, 'in the community'.

Of course, it would be wrong to argue that all moves against collective forms of care have been rooted simply in the ideological move to the right, as seen in recent years. There have been many who supported the running down of institutional care and the development of family-based care, while insisting at the same time that society must retain a collective responsibility for the support of that care. In terms of the distinctions discussed in Chapter 3, they do not disagree about the issue of responsibility but they do disagree on the matter of domain and form. Collectivists of whatever sort, however, do not believe that sturdy self-reliance and individual effort are sufficient formulae for the provision of decent standards of care in the community. As they know all too well, the moral concept of 'community spirit', as invoked by the right, rarely exists to solve the pressing, chronic, unrelenting problems thrown up, in reality, by community care policies, and the 'community spirit' often invoked by the left is a delicate plant that withers easily if not constantly watered and nourished by *collective* action. It is the unhappy combination of the individualist perspective, together with the view that sees care as being predominantly the responsibility of family, neighbours and volunteers, that leads logically to the inequitable outcomes of current community care policies.

When social care policies are under the direction of this sort of individualist philosophy, responsibility will increasingly be thrown on to those in most need of collectivist support: those who cannot provide care from their own resources, be they financial or comprising informal networks of relatives, friends and neighbours. It is crucial that those who support policies for closing down institutions do not align themselves with those individualist community care policies, the logical outcomes of which are the placing of greater burdens on families and the isolation of people within their own homes with only minimal professional support. It is beholden on opponents of such policies to consider what alternative options might be open to those wishing to see an end to the regimentation and insensitivity of institutional life but who nevertheless wish to see society taking collective responsibility for the care of those who are dependent. Those advocates of community care who would also argue the case for collective responsibility should look critically at the underlying assumptions upon which current policies are based and be prepared to accept that there is a logical and feasible case for extending collectivist principles into the spheres of form and domain.

In this context, it is appropriate to explore possible ways of adopting collective forms of care whereby society might fulfil its responsibility. Just as we may ask whether or not it is feasible to structure the social organization of daily living on a collective basis, so may we also pose the same question regarding the social organization of caring, both at the 'micro' level of individuals seeking practical solutions on a collective basis for the care of their dependants and at the 'macro' level of society adopting social policies that foster collectivist approaches on a wider scale.

Are there lessons to be learnt from elsewhere, from both the past and the present? Does the available evidence on alternative ways of organizing daily living shed any light on possible ways of organizing social care? Again, the evidence is variable, and a distinction must be made between formal and informal modes of care. One characteristic that most traditional societies have in common is, or was, the absence of a highly specialized division of labour, whereby specific categories of the population spend their lives in waged labour providing care for other categories of the population in separate locations. The same is also true for other forms of segregation that more complex societies use as a means of solving other social needs or problems, namely schools, for the education of children in preparation for life in wider society, and prisons, for the custody of criminally deviant people. All forms of caring, for the able-bodied (for example, young children) and for the sick alike, are, rather than being separated from mainstream society, integrated into the fabric of daily life.

Caring in traditional societies

The care of dependent people

Because there is relatively little specialized division of labour in traditional societies, caring becomes absorbed into a collectivity of functions, none of which, in a subsistence economy, is demarcated in terms of cash payments or by the public/private dichotomy. In addition, what has been termed the social construction of dependency is of a different order in such societies compared with its construction in capitalist societies. In the latter, those who cannot work (for wages) through physical or mental impairment, or those who have passed beyond the age limit imposed by society on the end of working life, automatically become dependent on either the state (for income maintenance and social and welfare support), their own thrift or their family. Their dependency is not intrinsic to their physical or 'chronological' condition; they have been 'socially constructed' as dependent because they are arbitrarily ruled out from being party to the bargain or contract that non-dependent individuals are able, or obliged, to enter into with society (that if you work in the public domain, you receive the wherewithal to sustain life). In traditional subsistence economies where the cash nexus is absent, those whom capitalist society would deem to be dependent are sometimes able to strike another form of contract.

Thus, in the case of the aged, the wisdom and experience that are deemed to accrete to old age might be highly valued, and such people, rather than being seen as dependent and redundant, are regarded as influential and powerful (Pelling and Smith, 1991). Many such societies might be classified as gerontocracies where old *men* have exclusive access to political power and primary access to the reproductive capacities of young women. Even in less extreme cases, old age may nevertheless be venerated and the elderly will be awarded extreme respect. The care of elderly people in these circumstances would be of a different order; it would be part of a continuing and reciprocal relationship between them and other sections of society. However, in either case, the physical dependency of old people would not be regarded as a handicap because they would be seen as valued – and powerful – members of society.

The position of younger, physically or mentally impaired people might be more precarious. All people get old, and as they do, the likelihood of dependency increases; it is usual, it is the norm. Youthful dependency (beyond childhood) through physical or mental impairment is, however, outside the norm. Dependent young people might be marginalized or excluded from society, perhaps seen as possessing ritual powers dangerous to 'normal' members and thus classified as malign influences, as witches, or simply pushed aside as non-human. On the other hand, there are well-known instances of the ritual powers attributed by a given society to physically or mentally impaired people being positively valued and incorporated into society – the North American shamans were an example of this.

The point to emphasize is that dependency and caring may be perceived differently in different societies. Systems of support and care may therefore vary according to the degree to which the confinements of chronic physical or mental disability are compounded by the social constraints of marginalization and stigmatization *or* mitigated by the social supports of integration and 'valuation'. This is not to say that in those societies where chronically infirm people are valued and integrated into society, there is no need for care to be provided.

How then do those societies that do not have formal segregated care systems go about the business of caring for their dependent members? The evidence suggests that it is the principle and structure of kinship that provide the basis for caring. Because kinship organization in small-scale societies is very often based on collectivist principles, caring too is integrated into this collectivist approach.

Many instances are cited in ethnographic literature of how elderly people are incorporated into the life of the wider kin group as they go through the process of ageing – the cyclical nature of life is recognized: people move through a series of stages, interlinked and predetermined. A widow may move into her own hut within the larger compound containing the huts of her children and their offspring, so that they will be able to tend her as necessary. In other cases, ageing parents may continue to live in the family home as they have always done with their children and their children's children, and gradually give up duties and responsibilities that were formerly theirs. In other settings, their jural status may be altered to accommodate their changing situation: customs such as the levirate require or enable an ageing woman on widowhood to become the wife of her dead husband's brother. Thus in societies where there is no jural or economic means of accommodating women on their own, their status is transferred so that they are not excluded from society. This obviously appears to be an extreme solution to those brought up in societies that have a more elaborate structure of roles and relationships, but it may be crucial in those where roles are more rigidly defined. Indeed, it might be argued that the very elaborateness and fluidity of those other societies often militates against those in transition. Because their changing status is unclear, it becomes ambiguous and more difficult for those individuals to find any solid basis upon which to define their new position. Although, in theory, the opportunities are there for them to reintegrate according to their individual circumstances, they more often become marginalized and devalued.

Of course, in many traditional societies, environmental conditions have been so severe that those people unable to play a full part in the economic life of the community, or who are too great a drain on its resources, are at a disadvantage. Thus it has been the practice, in certain cases, to abandon those who become or are likely to become chronically dependent in this way. Eskimos and some Native American tribes traditionally exposed aged people to die. In other societies, on the birth of twins, one or both might similarly have been exposed to die, partly because of the ritual dangerousness of twins, but also by reason of the extra burden placed on nursing mothers in contexts of malnourishment and environmental pressures. Direct action of this nature is not the only, or indeed the most likely, consequence of severe environmental conditions. People are simply less likely to survive into old age or to overcome severe illness at an earlier age. Thus there are likely to be far fewer individuals becoming chronically dependent and requiring social support from the community around them. Just as there have been an increasing number of dependent people surviving as a consequence of improvements in standards of living and medical technology in contemporary times in Western society (Illsley, 1981), so the reverse is true for traditional and Third World societies. Mortality rates are likely to be higher where there are lower standards of living and an absence of adequate medical care and public health measures.

The care of children

While there may be little evidence from traditional societies regarding the care of chronically sick and dependent people from which to learn, there is a wealth of information relating to the care of 'normally' dependent people, namely children. It is striking how frequently the rearing of children seems to be a collective enterprise in societies across the world. The jural relationship of parents and children may vary across societies, according to whether there are patrilineal or matrilineal modes of descent, which will govern the relationship between fathers and children or mother's brothers and children. The affective relationship may also vary: in some societies greater emphasis may be put on paternal roles in daily life than in others. However, it is clear that children in general are accurately aware of the nature of these relationships from a very early age, regardless of whether they are reared collectively on a day-to-day basis or not.

Even Bowlby (1984) in his work on attachment recognizes that this is so; likewise Spiro (1954), in his work on kibbutz-reared children, accepts this. Thus a collective form of childrearing can be seen as an *augmentation* of these basic and clearly defined relationships. However, Bowlby's work is full of confusions. He recognizes that collective care does not kill off the instinctive feelings of attachment of child to mother and also agrees that children are able, from an early age, to form attachments with other 'care-takers' besides the mother. At the same time, however, he links the overwhelming sense of loss, or detachment, on the removal of the mother directly to the child's being cared for 'collectively', in an institution such as a hospital or in a residential nursery. Furthermore, he argues that this sense of loss is not due to the 'pathological' circumstances of poor unloving institutional care but is directly due to the removal of the mother. He then cites as proof completely contradictory evidence. First, he instances a sense of loss being triggered by the removal of a mother-figure (not the real mother, who was in fact present during the critical period of the mother-figure's removal). Second, he quotes an example of similar distress being felt at the absence of real parents, although the child in question continued to be cared for in his normal surroundings by his normal care-takers (in a kibbutz) (Bowlby, 1984).

In the first case, he suggests that it is the removal of the regular care-taker, regardless of blood tie, that causes the distress; in the second, the regular care-takers remain, but the distress is caused by the removal of the blood-linked, non-care-taking parents. It is unclear on this evidence whether it is the bonding relationship brought about by continuous caring for, or the nature of the blood tie between mother and child that is seen by Bowlby as crucial. This confusion may simply point to the fact that it is dangerous to generalize from two cases separated by time and culture (the first case being reported from Germany in 1919 and the second from Israel after 1948). It also indicates the inaccurate and fallacious nature of many of Bowlby's arguments.

Another prime example occurs where he attempts to construct an evolutionary continuum of the nature of attachment, whereby in lower primates attachment is characterized by the instinctive ability of the offspring to cling to the mother, which is gradually replaced in the higher primates by the mother taking the initiative to keep the child in close proximity. This may be true, but the error that then follows is of dramatic proportions. He suggests that the same can be said for humans 'in the simpler societies' (side by side, therefore, on the continuum with gorilla mothers and babies), but in economically developed Western societies, he goes on to argue, mothers keep their children out of contact with them for many hours, even during the night (and this he criticizes). Apart from the danger of extrapolating from animals to human beings, he is also in danger of implying that biological evolution is at work differentiating 'simpler' human mothering habits from 'developed' human mothering habits – and that is the stuff not only of biological determinism, but also of racism.

The point of this digression is to indicate that the authority frequently cited as justifying certain childrearing practices is unreliable, both in terms of muddled basic concepts and the sorts of argument he employs. There are few who argue against the central significance of the mother – especially in physiological, hormonal terms immediately after the birth and then in early childhood – but to go on to conflate this, as he does, with other traumatic, atypical, culturally deviant events, such as the incarceration of children in unloving institutions, is wrong. What he fails to do is to examine how (and perhaps why) children are able to flourish and develop in collective situations (as it is known from the ethnographic and some contemporary evidence that they do), and at the same time maintain identification and warm affective links with their natural mothers (as he knows they do). However, perhaps the very fact that this culture regards the issue as a matter for surprise and investigation is simply a reflection on its atypical and peculiar approach to childrearing. It may be that it is familial ideology and not collective care that is the aberrant factor in all of this.

Certainly, the picture of young children being cared for by a number of people – both adults and older children, both kin and non-kin – is a familiar image across the world. The following passage from the classic anthropological text by Radcliffe-Brown (1964, p. 76), *The Andaman Islanders*, originally written almost ninety years ago, is typical of many other ethnographic accounts written subsequently:

> Children are such favourites with the Andamanese that a child is played with and petted and nursed not only by his own father and mother but by everyone in the village. A woman with an unweaned child will often give suck to the children of other women... Before the children can walk they are carried about by the mother and sometimes by the father or other persons.

In the case of the Andaman Islanders, it was commonplace for children to be fostered into the families of friends and neighbours. Radcliffe-Brown quotes the evidence of an earlier European visitor to the islands, a Mr Man, who observed similar practices himself. Once children had reached the age of six or seven, they frequently moved to live with other families and their own parents took in children from elsewhere. There was no apparent economic reason for doing this; it was simply a means of fulfilling friendship obligations. It did not mean that their parental or filial feelings were diminished; these ties were maintained by frequent visiting. Thus the day-to-day caregiving became vested in non-kin, but affective and jural relationships between parents and children were maintained.

Fostering has been commonplace too in many other parts of the world – that is, fostering in the sense that parents do not regard themselves as having *exclusive* rights over the rearing of their children, and therefore perceive a variety of benefits to stem from the 'sharing' of these with other people. Goody's (1982) study of fostering practices in

West Africa demonstrates that it is widespread there and relates its different forms to the structures of the particular societies involved. Thus those societies broadly characterized as non-centralized, segmentary and acephalous in structural terms are less inclined to adopt the practice, or if they do, do so only amongst close kin. On the other hand, more differentiated, centralized societies have adopted elaborate forms of the practice. In some cases, it may be to cement alliances and friendships, in others it may be to offer informal training and learning opportunities, or it may be to acquire more formal skills (in the manner of apprenticeships), or to enable children concerned to be better placed economically and socially in their future lives.

These practices may seem strange to those raised in the normative framework of Western culture, in which parents cling to their rights of possession over their children and where they regard the socialization and training of their children as both their exclusive duty and function. However, as Goody (1982, p. 34) says, there are other ways of perceiving these reciprocal, intergenerational roles and duties:

> Because in our own society parental roles are largely concentrated and are regarded as most appropriately filled by the biological parents within the nuclear family, we tend to see this constellation as both right and necessary. Yet these roles are potentially available for sharing not only among kin but even with unrelated neighbours, with friends or with the state. Sharing is one way of spreading the task of caring for deprived children. But it is also an effective way of forging links between adults – parent and pro-parent – and between generations – child and parent, child and pro-parent. Where sharing of parental roles is institutionalised, as in the giving of foster-children and in ritual sponsorship, such links are systematically created. To understand these simply as ways of coping with crisis situations, or of arranging to cope with them should they occur, is to fail to recognise the way in which many societies make use of the unique strength of the bonds between parent and children.

Historically, in Western societies, varieties of this less exclusive approach have also been known. Fostering as a means of conducting apprenticeships was a practice widespread in medieval Europe, as was that of wet-nursing, whereby the parental role of nurturance, as Goody terms it, as opposed to that of training, was delegated to other women, although it should be noted that this latter custom was by no means a benign practice for either the working-class women who performed it or for the children, according to accounts of the period (Flandrin, 1979).

Clearly the development of such customs in the past must bear some relation to contemporary conceptions of childhood and the relationship between parents and children. A number of sources have suggested that there was no conception of childhood *per se* and that children were simply viewed as miniature adults. Others have contested this view, arguing that children have always been seen as children by parents and society alike (Pollock, 1983). Further research may confirm the validity of one or other view, but in the meantime it is enough to conclude that all societies need to have some mechanisms and structures within which children can be nurtured, socialized in its broadest sense (to be brought up as members of society) and trained (to perform the specific tasks required for survival and subsistence).

Historical evidence

Collective responsibility

Society in preindustrial England has been characterized as fundamentally individualist, the nuclear family being the 'building brick' upon which wider structures were based. In this case, it is apposite to ask how dependent members were cared for in the past, given that there was no large-scale public sector staffed by a special-ized workforce to provide care, and given the proposition that the basic units of social organization were small nuclear families, split off from the wider extended family network. The evidence from traditional societies suggests that where there is no specialized division of labour, the extended network of kinship relationships provides the structure of support. Preindustrial society in England was characterized by a growing specialization in the division of labour (the development of craft gilds, the growth of towns and the landless labouring class is evidence of this). What mechanisms were available for the provision of care and support – especially for the poor – in this context, where infirm elderly, young and chronically disabled people would have found it difficult to maintain any independent existence?

There are two immediate possible responses: first, that there were institutions – notably the Church – that could provide the equivalent of 'public sector' social care and support, and second, that extended groups of kin did not have to live under the same roof to be able to take responsibility for the care of dependent kin. This latter is the case that Greer (1985) makes in her attack on Laslett. She suggests that families did not have to live under one roof in order to feel kinship obligations. Finch (1995), in relation to contemporary Britain, makes a related point, suggesting the concept of kinship *commitments* rather than kinship obligations – relationships of reciprocal caring and support negotiated and developed over time between particular sets of relations. Whatever the actuality of kinship dynamics in the preindustrial period, any consideration of who cared and how care was accomplished raises fundamental questions, one related to demography and the other related to social policy or perhaps political philosophy.

First, the demographic question: how many people were actually in a position to care; how many people needed to be cared for? And thence, were the mechanisms for caring of central or peripheral importance in social terms? Was it seen as a significant social issue? While the twentieth century has seen a spectacular leap in the proportion of elderly people in the population – 15.9 per cent of those aged over 65 in 1991, compared with 4.7 per cent in 1901 (Grundy, 1995) – the population was, during the nineteenth century, by and large a young one, an outcome determined by rates of fertility rather than by life expectancy (R. M. Smith, 1984). Between 1801 and 1851, for example, the proportion of elderly people (over 60 years old) in the population was at its lowest point in recorded time, at around 7 per cent, compared with 10 per cent at the beginning of the eighteenth century. Smith suggests that while the proportion for the present day is remarkable, there is no reason to suppose that the English population right back to the Middle Ages was not characterized by fluctuations in its demographic structure, allied to such factors as late marriage and changes in fertility rates. Thus it is mistaken to base perceptions of the size of the elderly population in past times solely on the number of elderly people in the nineteenth-century population.

From this, he goes on to argue that the burden of caring would also have varied accordingly. Thus when the proportion of elderly people was high, as in the late seventeenth century, there were relatively fewer children to be supported; therefore the overall burden of caring may have been reduced. However, when other demographic factors, such as late marriage – allied with the incontrovertible evidence of the 'nuclear family residence rule' (J. E. Smith, 1984) – are taken into account, the problem of how those elderly people were cared for, in financial and economic terms, as well as tending in times of infirmity, remains. Laslett (Laslett and Wall, 1972), in spite of what Greer claims, has suggested that non-cohabiting kin would have been available to support them, but J. E. Smith argues that this would have been especially difficult during the preindustrial period. Nuclear family-based households would have had difficulty in accumulating any form of savings over and above what was expended to meet the needs of day-to-day living and the exigencies of bad harvests, unemployment and illness within the household unit itself. There would have been little possibility of building surpluses that could be transferred to the households of others in times of dependency. Coupled with this, it was likely that elderly people would be the greatest burden at precisely the time when young households were at their greatest point of strain in structural terms. Because the custom was to leave the parental household on marriage, young married couples (marrying late according to the norm) were unlikely to have accumulated sufficient assets from which to transfer support to the parental household they had just left, at the time when that household needed it most. As R. M. Smith (1984, p. 425) says:

> Where marriage is late, as it was historically in North West Europe, the parents of married couples began to lose their children's earnings and to lose each other in widowhood precisely at the point in their children's own life course when these children were themselves liable to be in poverty because of their own offspring.

According to recent evidence, those who were in need of social and financial support – old people and widows in particular – did find the care they needed during the preindustrial period and, contrary to what has commonly been supposed, they were cared for through collective responsibility. Examination of parish records is beginning to reveal the extent to which local parishes made resources available to those in need within their boundaries (and within their criteria of residential eligibility). Studies of widowhood indicate that during the eighteenth century, for example, high proportions of widows in those parishes under examination maintained their own households rather than being taken into the households of others (J. E. Smith, 1984).

Smith hypothesizes that there were perhaps two opposing means whereby they might have been able to do this: first, that they were supported in their own homes from their own resources and by those children who still lived with them, and second, that they were maintained in their own households by support from a variety of external sources – the kin of the widow and of the deceased husband, informal charitable assistance from neighbours, landlords, and so on, formal charity such as parish relief, or privately managed charity. He suggests that the latter was most likely and cites evidence from a study of the records of a number of parishes taken from a period between 1695 and 1796. While one fifth of households were in receipt of parish relief (a high proportion in itself), twice that proportion of widow-headed households were 'on the parish'. He also concludes that it was widowhood *per se* that accounted for this proportion, rather than other factors. He suggests:

> that in pre-industrial society, where becoming a widow and especially a widow with dependent children was a likelihood and where remarriage was more a prerogative of men than women, the parish necessarily stepped in to provide life support for widows and their children. (J. E. Smith, 1984)

The records of certain London parishes in the seventeenth century have been examined to try to determine what public mechanisms were available for the provision of care for sick people of the parish (Wear, 1986). Again, at this stage, the amount of evidence available is relatively slight, but it seems to indicate that there were well-developed systems of collective responsibility for the care of the parish sick, at least by the seventeenth century. Substantial sums were seen to be spent by the parish in paying individuals to nurse sick people, even paying family members to care for sick relatives. The point Wear makes in particular is that there seemed to be a system of welfare by contract developing. The parish authorities did not force families to care; they paid sums of money to facilitate their caring, where that was possible. Furthermore, the collective responsibility taken by the parish to support its sick poor was an altruistic act, in the sense that the parish was prepared to support those who were sick and who had little chance of recovery or rehabilitation.

This leads to questions of political and social philosophy. The accepted wisdom until recently has frequently suggested that, in preindustrial societies, those in need fell back on the support of their families. Only *in extremis* did the Church or the parish have to step in, revealing an implicit assumption of the strength of the extended kinship network. Current studies are beginning to suggest the opposite: that far from the collectivity taking on the role of residual support, it has rather taken on a central role in England and in other areas of north-west Europe since at least the Middle Ages. As R. M. Smith (1984, p. 423) says:

> From a very early period in English history, and in other North-West European areas, it seems that 'risk devolution' and poor relief have been centred on the community rather than on the family. While particular institutional arrangements have varied over time – with the source of relief, for example, shifting from manors and gilds to parish, to Poor Law Union and eventually to the state itself – there has nevertheless been a remarkable consistency in the extra-familial locus of welfare institutions.

The issue of the relationship between collectivism and individualism, which is familiar to feminists and other students of social policy today, seems to have been around for a long time. Likewise, concern for the fate of the poor and the dependent has been apparent for as long, as has the debate about who exactly comprise the poor and dependent. R. M. Smith (1984) quotes Tierney as noting that the canonists and decretists of the twelfth century were as concerned with pronouncing on these issues as were the commentators of the nineteenth century – Arthington, Dalton, Booth and Rowntree – and those of today. Clay, writing in 1909, cites a proclamation from 1359 as evidence of this. Vagrants were deemed to be unworthy of support; they were 'such unworthy beggars [who] do waste divers alms, which would otherwise be given to many poor folks, such as lepers, blind, halt and persons oppressed with old age and divers other maladies'.

The very fact that society, be it in the guise of its formal institutions or its learned commentators, has been concerned to determine the division between deserving and undeserving – however just or unjust its conclusions may have been at any given time – indicates that responsibility for that category that was deemed to be eligible (deserving) was seen to belong to society as a whole. It was not simply a question of its being left to the arbitrariness of private charity, although the point at which the division (between deserving and undeserving) was made perhaps indicates the extent of society's willingness to take collective responsibility at any given time. Interestingly, R. M. Smith (1984, p. 422) suggests that demographic pressures might have had something to do with this:

> Without wishing to impose a sense of demographic determinism on these issues, it is worth noting that the more 'individualistic' or family-oriented solutions proposed in the treatment of the elderly were during phases such as the later sixteenth and early seventeenth centuries and again in the nineteenth century. These were times when the welfare claims on the communal funds were very pressing. Our understanding of witchcraft accusations in the matter of the elderly and the supposed guilt of children and neighbours in late Tudor and early Stuart England with regard to their treatment of elderly women is certainly extended by these considerations. So also are the reduction of out-relief and the attempts to cajole children under legal threat to care for or contribute to the cost of care for their parents in the nineteenth century.

Thomson (1983, 1991), however, places less emphasis on demographic factors in his discussion of the treatment of elderly people in the late nineteenth century. He suggests that it was less a question of the total amount of resources available, and more a matter of society's moral choices about how to distribute them across society.

However the balance of provision varied over time, collective support was always available. Himmelfarb (1985) notes how visitors to England at various times in the preindustrial or early industrial past were impressed (for good or ill) by the extent to which English society felt responsible for the social conditions of the poor. She quotes Franklin in 1766:

> There is no country in the world where so many provisions are established for them; so many hospitals to receive them when they are sick and lame, founded and maintained by voluntary charities; so many almshouses for the aged of both sexes, together with a solemn law made by the rich to subject their estates to a heavy tax for the support of the poor. (Himmelfarb, 1985, p. 5)

Equally, de Tocqueville whom she quotes was of the same view:

> The majority of the English having all these things (clean clothes, healthy foods, comfortable quarters) regard their absences as a frightful

misfortune; society believes itself bound to come to the aid of those who
lack them and cures evils which are not even recognised elsewhere. In
England the average standard of living man can hope for in the course
of his life is higher than in any other country of the world. (Himmelfarb, 1985, p. 148)

However, both visitors felt this was detrimental. Franklin ended
his observation thus:

In short, you offered a premium for the encouragement of idleness, and
you should not now wonder that it has had its effect in the increase of
poverty.

and de Tocqueville:

This greatly facilitates the extension of pauperism in that kingdom.

It was attitudes like these that fuelled the debate surrounding the
reform of the old Poor Law in 1834 and which determined the shape of
the New Poor Law with its emphasis on less eligibility, the cutting down
on outdoor relief and the consequent concentration of the needy (of all
categories) into the institutional framework of the workhouse.

Thomson (1983) takes up this theme in his study of elderly people
during the Victorian period and suggests that there have been long-
term consequences. Careful analysis of the incomes of both elderly
and non-elderly households over the last century and a half show that
the elderly fared better up till the middle of the nineteenth century,
relative to the non-elderly, than at any time since. While the New
Poor Law was passed in 1834, in which responsibility was expected to
pass from the community to individuals and families, it was not
implemented to take effect as far as elderly people were concerned
until the period after 1860. Up until that point, the earlier system of
pensions being paid out on a regular basis to a majority of working-
class elderly people was maintained, regardless of their family
situation. The level of those pensions was, Thomson reckons, around
70 per cent of the average income of a working-class household.

Elsewhere, reinforcing this point, Thomson (1991) refers to one
local area that he has studied in some detail – Ampthill in Bedford-
shire – which he characterizes as having been profligate in the
generosity with which it handed out poor relief in the eighteenth

century. Even though it came under the control of 'enthusiastic devotees of the newly fashionable principles, which held that responsibility in welfare matters was to be shifted back from the community to the individual and the family' (p. 200), Thomson says that, after a handful of cases immediately after 1834, not a single case was recorded between 1840 and the late 1860s of children being handed down parent maintenance orders. This was in contrast to a steady flow of prosecutions of parents of young children. During the same period, 500 elderly people (the total population of Ampthill being 16 000, of whom 1 000 were elderly) were regularly maintained on a continuous basis out of poor relief funds.

After the 1860s, the general position worsened. Poor Law pensions were slashed and often withdrawn, and the plight of working-class elderly people became the focus of political concern, leading to the introduction of the National Insurance pension scheme in 1911. Even after the new scheme, and likewise after 1945, the value of pensions relative to the average working-class income has never reached the earlier levels, even when the hidden value of spending on health and welfare services in the present period is taken into account. Thomson reckons that nowadays the old age pensioner's income in Britain (from all sources) is around 40 per cent of the average working-class income. Moreover, Thomson directly relates the fall in pensioner incomes at particular periods to the increase in the numbers of elderly people entering residential care, particularly in the latter half of the nineteenth century and, to a certain extent, in the present period, and to the shift in the balance from a predominantly male residential population to a female one.

An examination of the extent and variety of sources of collective financial support for older people during the nineteenth century makes for a sobering reappraisal of current debates about support for the aged. A majority of older people were supported by poor law pensions: Thomson cites a figure of over half for the elderly population of Barton-upon-Irwell, Lancashire and, in the 1840s in Ampthill, two in every three women over 70 and one out of every two men of the same age group. In addition to this, according to Thomson, around 10 per cent of men past the age of 60 were likely to have been in receipt of a war pension, and between 1 and 2 per cent of older men received other government allowances or superannuations. Furthermore, in some places, 10 per cent of elderly women lived in charity housing of some form (probably 5 per cent across the whole country). In trying to assess levels of collective support during the past two or three hundred years, Thomson goes on to suggest that, in the past, up to 5 per cent of national income was redistributed in one form or another to the poor, compared with a mere 1 per cent at the beginning of this century and 3 per cent later on. Although it has moved beyond 6 per cent since the 1960s, this includes payments to relatively well-off people who receive payments not by virtue of their poverty, but because of age and family circumstances.

How does this evidence fit the commonly held perceptions of the respective roles of collective and familial responsibility for the care of the dependent in past times? Not well, it would appear. In certain schools of thought (Baker, 1979), there has been a tendency to see the development of social policy as a progressive ameliorating process, with the inception of the welfare state confirming and further developing those progressive trends. Thus it is difficult from that perspective to recognize that there has not been a unilinear, incremental improvement in 'welfare' – that is, in this context, in the willingness of the collectivity (be it the state, the municipality, the parish or whatever) to take responsibility for its members according to need rather than desert. Thus the base from which the welfare state sprang in the mid-twentieth century was itself a decline from a base of provision in an earlier period. R. M. Smith (1984) has indeed suggested that the growth in the socialist and feminist movements of the late nineteenth century might be directly linked to the withdrawal of support for the poor and the elderly in the middle of that century, as a result of the New Poor Law. A more common view, however, has been that current provision is the summation of a struggle for collectivist strategies over the decades and thus (according to the leftist view) an improvement upon that which went before. The threat that is perceived today – emanating from the new right – must, in that case, be a threat that has, *uniquely*, a possibility of setting back that progress. The idea that the position of the poor and the old has swung backwards and forwards during different periods does not conveniently fit this view.

For those on the right, the present conjuncture of forces presents an opportunity to regain some of the high ground of a golden age in the past when, according to their picture of that time, the virtues of sturdy self-reliance and individual responsibility held sway. Those are the 'Victorian values' of the new right, but there is a wealth of evidence to demonstrate that the application of those values (as seen in the swingeing consequences of the New Poor Law – Thomson [1991], for example, suggesting that between 1870 and the end of the century, public spending on old people was cut by at least one third) produced high numbers of casualties rather than a citizenry well disciplined in self-sufficiency. Victorian society itself provided many exceptions to the rule of single-minded self-interest. It was remarkable, for example, for its municipal approaches to public health, and it was a period that saw vast amounts of public money being set aside to build the large-scale institutions for the care of mentally ill and mentally disabled people that have been inherited today. While it might be said that the building of such large-scale institutions – set apart from the rest of society, around which veils of privacy could be drawn – says more about the character and attitudes of Victorian society than it does about its sense of altruism, the fact that society as a collective whole saw fit to make that provision its particular responsibility is worth noting.

It is also worth observing that all this took place during a period when an ideology of individualism, linked closely to the development of capitalism and the bourgeois nuclear family, would logically see solutions to the problem of caring as lying within the domestic sphere. Conversely, in the current postwar period, there has been a growing emphasis on individualist family-based solutions to care, in spite of the collectivist ethos engendered by the advent of the welfare state. As R. M. Smith (1984) says, 'we are obliged to ask why there existed this dialectical relationship between collectivism and individualism (or perhaps what might be termed as reluctant 'familism') in the matter of the support of the elderly in the English past and also the present'. It is perhaps a question of continual and continuous competition between ideologies that are pulling against each other that finds concrete expression in this variation of social forms. Although individualism has been dominant down the ages, the pull towards the collectivist alternative has always survived – often successfully. Feminists should take heart; the impulse that moves society to take collective responsibility for its members continues to survive and can be built on.

Of course, the existence of collective care in the past does not necessarily suggest that the *form* of care was at all times, or at any time, satisfactory. It is necessary to distinguish between collective provision (that is, the collectivity taking *responsibility* to provide) and collective *forms* of care. To report approvingly of collective responsibility may not imply approval of the form or standard of what was provided. It would be foolish for feminists to go down the road of giving approval for all that is worst in large-scale institutional care. It is likely that unless the issues of value, exploitation and discrimination (the moral status of those being cared for, the gendered division of labour relating to those who care both privately and publicly and the low economic value given to those who provide social care) are confronted, collective forms of social (non-private) care will continue to remain problematic.

Collective forms

It is difficult to assess the standards and style of care provided, historically, by collective means. When standards had deteriorated and when there were moves afoot to change policy, institutional care was likely to (but not necessarily) come in for criticism; equally, when institutional care was regarded as acceptable and standards were adequate, it might raise little comment. However, the question of why society, or certain groups within it, should become interested in the provision of care for particular groups at particular times remains – as noted earlier – unclear. It may be more to do with ideological attitudes towards what model of care is deemed to be appropriate at any given time than with practical issues such as standards of care. The paramouncy given to the values of independence and privacy in the present period over the benefits of residential living, regardless of how frail and isolated the person might be, may be a case in point.

Early forms of collective provision were to be seen in the growth of hospitals and almshouses in the medieval period. Woodward (1974) says that the first authenticated hospital – the Hospital of St Peter at York – was founded by the canons of York Minster in AD 947. It is likely that it served more as a hostel for wayfarers and pilgrims at its inception, only gradually taking on the role of nursing and tending the sick, as did other hospitals of the time. He names St Bartholomew's, founded in 1123, as the first hospital recognizable by today's standards, but Abel-Smith (1964) suggests that it was not really until the eighteenth century that the idea of founding hospitals specifically for the care of the sick, rather than for a mix of clientele, finally took hold, with the establishment of the voluntary hospital movement. However, over the centuries there were, undoubtedly, many institutions established that provided for the sick and needy by offering shelter and care on a collective basis. In a study of the development of hospitals in Europe, Thompson and Goldin (1975, p. 345) state:

> that towards the end of the Middle Ages, it was not uncommon for persons of moderate substance to arrange a kind of old-age insurance for themselves by signing over their property to a charitable foundation in return for board, lodging and medical care for the remainder of their lives.

They refer to them as 'superannuated pensioners'.

Almshouses built for group living by Churches, municipally controlled charitable institutions, private endowments and gilds have existed for many centuries, up until the present day. Certain sources emphasize the distinction between almshouses and hospitals. Godfrey (1955) describes in great detail the style and scope of almshouse building up to the eighteenth century. He notes that their building carried on until recent times, although they suffered two periods of recession, one when many were dissolved by King Edward VI, and the second during the nineteenth century when many of their resources were diverted for educational purposes by the Charity Commissioners. They provided sheltered accommodation for elderly people of all sorts – the craft gilds offered care for their aged members, and other foundations provided shelter for such categories as retired servants, discharged soldiers and sailors, distressed gentlefolk and the like. However, as Godfrey (1955, p. 19) notes, 'the majority of institutions [hospitals and almshouses], in the earlier centuries, were the natural centres for help to those in need who lived in the neighbourhood and to all poor travellers and wayfarers'.

Clay (1909) records that while many almshouses were set up for life-pensioners, others were established to serve more temporary or emergency needs. Such needs changed over time – the decline in leprosy and legislation inhibiting vagrancy affecting the make-up of the resident population – and many of these eventually became old-age homes.

During the eighteenth century, legislation was passed authorizing parishes to establish workhouses for the indigent and their families, and to provide them with work to cut the costs of providing for them.

In 1782 adjacent parishes were permitted to combine to provide workhouses for the exclusive use of children, the aged and the sick. Thus, by the nineteenth century, care for such categories was provided for by a variety of residential institutions – hospitals, almshouses, workhouses and the like – as noted by visiting commentators. Provision was variable across the country as were, no doubt, conditions within the establishments. This pattern of provision changed after the New Poor Law was passed in 1834, when, in spite of recommendations to the contrary, little differentiation was made between the sick and the able-bodied in eligibility and receipt of relief.

It is no part of the argument that favours collective forms of provision to suggest a return to the past, nor to suggest that conditions experienced by the sick and the poor in the past were necessarily acceptable or of a high standard. It is useful, however, to point out that collective provision (both in terms of responsibility for and the form of care provided) has a long and often worthy history, although at different times the degree to which the collectivity has been prepared to accept responsibility might have varied, and the standards of care provided might have fluctuated. There is no doubt, however, that considerable resources, commitment, pride and care have at certain times been allotted to the cause of collective provision. It is only necessary to look at the style and scale of the buildings constructed as hospitals for the sick, the elderly and the mentally ill to realize what major undertakings they must have been. The only other buildings of comparable size were either churches and other religious foundations or palaces and aristocrats' country houses. Thompson and Goldin (1975) quote a verse written at the time of the reconstruction of Bethlem:

> This is a structure fair
> Royally raised
> The pious founders are
> Much to be praised
> That in this time of need
> When sickness doth exceed
> Do build this house of bread
> Noble new Bedlam

They go on to recount its sad decline a hundred years later, saying, 'Hospitals have a way of being conceived in glory, executed with ingenuity and humanity, then subjected in use to misuse and abuse, finally to be overcrowded and understaffed and always and forever plagued by insufficient funds' (Thompson and Goldin, 1995, p. 345).

As they say, the models for these buildings were, variously, palaces, mansions and substantial private residences. Although their study is written as a critique of past hospital architecture – seeing it as a progressive process of development from the grandiose, large-scale institution (bad) to the small-scale, private, single-bed roomed hospital of modern day USA (good) – the size of the commitment involved in these earlier large-scale enterprises nevertheless shines through. It was only later in the history of each institution that conditions began to deteriorate, in comparison with both earlier and contemporary standards of domestic living. However, in the gloom, there were 'centres of excellence' in collective forms of care. The elegance of the building in which the famous Quaker initiative, the Retreat at York, was established in 1814, along with its trail-blazing methods of care and treatment, was outstanding. William Tuke, its founder, advocated the abolition of restraint in the treatment of his residents; they were encouraged to participate in everyday life and to follow ordinary everyday routines (although according to their class position). He provided a pattern for later policies, which, for its time, was exemplary.

While many have argued or assumed that the family was invariably the locus for caring in preindustrial times, and that sick and dependent people only resorted to institutional forms of social care in times of extreme destitution, it is likely that such care has historically played a greater part in relation to both the destitute and comfortably off alike than has hitherto been acknowledged (Jones, 1972). Even in the case of the well-to-do, care may indeed have been provided within the home, but the homes of the rich were themselves small-scale collective units, comprising kin, colleagues, friends and servants and it is unlikely that the burden of caring fell on nuclear family members themselves. In addition, there is frequent mention of ill-houses, which seemed to be something akin to small nursing homes, where those who could afford it booked themselves in for a fee for care and treatment. As for the poor, the role of the parish in supporting the sick and dependent – by providing institutional care (of varying standards) or pensions, or by paying for care and treatment – was not inconsiderable.

Ways of viewing the past

There are perhaps a number of accepted but mutually conflicting pictures of the pattern of caring in past times. One is the picture of the golden age: that in the generalized past (probably assumed to be pre-twentieth century), families cared for their dependent members. In preindustrial times it would have been the extended family, and in industrial Victorian Britain the archetypal, individualist nuclear family. Only in modern times are families supposedly unprepared to care.

Second is a modification of the first view: that only in the preindustrial past did families truly care, and that it was with the advent of capitalism and the introversion characteristic of the nuclear family and the breakdown of natural communities, together with the anomie and alienation that accompanied this, that dependent people were thrown on to the harsh mercy of the state and its institutional provision – because families would and could no longer care.

Third is the further view that there have been distinct phases in the provision of care, the earliest being that provided by the extended family in precapitalist society, which was supplanted by the harsh, uncaring institutional provision of the capitalist nineteenth century, and that this is now being replaced by a more caring form of community provision because of the enlightened process of social policy development.

The evidence briefly examined here suggests that all three pictures are incorrect. First, there was no such period as a golden age when community and family ideals at their warmest and cosiest reigned supreme. Second, the divide between preindustrial and industrial, capitalist society was not characterized by distinct and different forms and levels of collective responsibility and provision. Third, British society over many centuries has established substantial levels of collective responsibility and provision, and the twentieth century, when seen against this background, does not stand out clearly as pre-eminent in its willingness to take collective responsibility for its weakest members. In absolute terms, current standards and levels of provision are obviously greater than in past times, but as proportions of total available resources for social redistribution, comparatively, over time, they may not be so. Indeed, the current period is perhaps showing a clearer tension between the private and the collective than earlier times. There is ideological pressure for the narrow-focused, isolated nuclear family unit to be seen as the normative model (even though not in practice). Yet this is coupled with a trend towards the growth in numbers of small, fragmented household units – more people living on their own, the size of houses greatly diminished, early completion of childbearing – as distinct from the larger households of the past, which were composed, in Victorian times at least, of a mixture of nuclear family members, servants and lodgers of various types. Thus the modern family is in a worse position to provide care than ever it was in the past, and there is greater pressure put upon it, in terms of official policy and normative attitudes, to provide that care.

The potential for social care, through collective means, has varied over the centuries, and it is by no means clear that current provision under the welfare state is as proportionately generous in terms of the share of collective resources devoted to it as that in past times. In spite of some commonly held assumptions about the extent of kinship relationships in the preindustrial past, collectively provided care was available and kinfolk were not expected to care on a purely altruistic basis. Likewise with the advent of urban, capitalist society, the development of the bourgeois values associated with privatized, individualist nuclear family life were accompanied by a massive and costly investment in social care at its most institutional. This seeming contradiction is mirrored conversely in the present period by current policies seeking to push care back into the privatized, individualist nuclear family, although the welfare state is technically supposed to offer care from the cradle to the grave. The relationship of ideology to social structure and social policies is thus more subtle and ambiguous than polemicists are ready to recognize. The conclusion to draw from this variety of evidence is perhaps to take notice of the past but not to assume that currently held views of what went before are necessarily correct. Today's pictures of the past generally seek to confirm and validate policies of the present.

6

The principles and practice of collective care

If contemporary community care policies have the effect of placing an unacceptable burden of care on families – and the evidence suggests that they do – alternatives must be considered. An obvious candidate, according to the argument developed here, is the collective or communal alternative. In earlier chapters, the part played by collectivist structures in daily life and in the provision of care has been considered. The conclusions drawn from this are somewhat tentative and patchy. Broadly speaking, it has been suggested that there are examples of collective forms existing and persisting successfully through time, but they have mostly been imperfect, especially when viewed from a feminist perspective. It has also been argued that collectivist impulses to care for the dependent have figured prominently over time in contention with more dominant individualistic urges. Thus society has frequently been able to act upon its sense of collective responsibility for the care of its weaker members. It is this fundamental tendency that should be consolidated and built upon. Furthermore, collectivism, as it relates to the three component parts discussed earlier – responsibility, form and domain – should provide the basis for a comprehensive framework for caring. As we know, this treads on dangerous territory; while many would agree with the view that collectivism implies a collective *responsibility* at a general level, far fewer would agree that it can extend into the private domain of caring to replace the familial model of care.

In this context, how would the collective alternative work out? It is important to establish fundamental principles against which alternative options might be measured. It is a relatively straightforward

121

matter to identify those characteristics of existing institutional or residential care which constitute bad standards of care; it is more difficult to identify those which constitute high standards. In the case of bad standards, the effects that Townsend (1962) refers to are the characteristics to beware of – lack of privacy, lack of personal relationships, the 'defensive shell of isolation', restricted mobility and access to wider society and social segregation of staff and residents. Additional characteristics to guard against are routines organized around the needs of the institution and/or its staff instead of around its residents (early waking, conveyor belt-type care – all washed together, all fed together, all put to bed together, and so on).

Good residential care (one form of collective care) is more difficult to characterize, partly because one of the most fundamental principles upon which it should be based is a capacity for flexibility and respon- siveness to individual needs. So collective forms of care do not necessarily mean the varieties of residential care that are familiar to most people today; they certainly do not imply the vast institutional establishments of the past. Size and scale might not, in some cases, differ very greatly from those current residential settings, but the style of care within them might differ vastly. Good collective care is less to do with size and numbers than it is to do with the style and content of care and of the relationships of people involved in them – both carers and cared for. For example, *Home Life*, a code of practice for residen- tial care published in 1984 (Centre for Policy on Ageing, 1994) and updated in 1996, outlines a set of principles that should underpin good care: fulfilment, individuality, dignity, autonomy, respect and esteem. These provide a useful starting point for developing a coherent and principled approach to organizing residential care.

Essential principles of collective care

Building on this approach, it is possible to identify further essential principles that must be observed in the development of any form of care. Responsiveness to individual need and inclination is clearly one, but perhaps overriding that and all others from the cared-for person's perspective is the ability for that person to be responsible for his or her own life. This is a theme that emerges from many studies of disability and dependence (Blaxter, 1976; Shearer, 1982a; Morris, 1991, 1993), and it is precisely this quality that current provision too often denies. Disabled people recognize quite clearly that, to varying degrees, they require assistance or support (Morris, 1991; Wood, 1991) from other people for the performing of certain basic tasks. They acknowledge that independence, in the sense that this might imply freedom from such reliance on other people, is not an option for them, however sophisticated mechanical aids and adaptations might become. What they are concerned with is to be able to control the way in which they manage that dependence and the degree to which they have options from which to choose. Dependence and interdependence are a part of ordinary life (Shearer, 1982b); a life of total *independence* would mean isolation and separation. In the view of one disabled person, disabled people are victims of an 'ideology of independence' whereby a disabled person is penalized by exclusion from society if he or she is unable to accomplish the tasks of daily living; for the disabled person, independence means *control* rather than accomplishment of this kind (Brisenden, 1989, quoted in Morris, 1993).

For collectivists, it is the recognition of dependence and interdependence as facets of all human relationships that validates their approach to the issue of caring. By the collectivity taking on responsibility for the provision of care, the tensions, burden and obligation inherent in the one-to-one caring relationship, which are the product of the family model of care, are overcome. Particular individuals are not forced into particular caring and cared for roles, dictated by their social and biological relatedness, for it is in those relationships that dependence becomes a warped and unhealthy pressure on the actors involved. In collectively shared relationships of caring, the burdens are dispersed and fewer pressures arise. The individuals who are being cared for are not forced into dependence on certain other individuals with whom they might have other kinds of relationships (of love, dislike, intellectual partnership, parenthood, siblingship, and so on).

Thus the first principle of collective care, which is also applicable to any form of care provision, must be for the disabled and/or dependent individual to be in a position to be responsible for his or her life choices. These should not be once-and-for-all choices – the possibility for change has to be incorporated. Equally, those who provide care should also be in a position to be responsible for decisions about their role in providing care. Women should not be forced into the position of having to care at the cost of other choices, and the status and economic rewards of caring should be comparable with those of alternative activities.

A second principle should be that the system of care should be responsive to the needs and inclinations of the individuals receiving care. This must mean that forms of care should be flexible in themselves – rigid routines and fixed expectations should play no part – and movement between different forms of care *when appropriate* should be possible. However, this should not be mandatory; concepts such as the continuum of care, which sees dependent people moving from one form of care into another as their dependency-related conditions improve or deteriorate, often fail to recognize the regimentation which that may involve. Existing care should be responsive, as far as possible, to accommodate such changes, rather than the dependent person being expected to change location.

A third principle must be maximal opportunity to form as wide and varied a range of personal relationships as the individual might wish. This might be coupled with a fourth principle – an equally maximal opportunity to develop skills and talents in any way that the individual chooses. It is important to recognize the multiplicity of skills and talents that every individual has and – in the case of older people – has developed and nurtured over a lifetime. Room must also be given for the expression of joy and sorrow and for the capacity for intimacy (Brown and Thompson, 1994). These principles relate closely to concepts of integration, ordinary life and normalization, although the normative and, indeed, prescriptive implications of the latter concept may be inappropriate (Dalley, 1992) if one of the objects of this alternative approach to care is to open up new ways of being and doing. Dependent individuals should not be cut off from other areas of social life if they choose not to be; on the other hand, they should be free to develop their own social environment in the way they wish. An ordinary life means precisely that – that the lives of dependent people should be unremarkable, should not be *ab*normal.

A fifth principle should underwrite all the others: dependent people should be economically secure, to ensure that the other principles have real meaning. Berthoud (1991), Shearer (1982a) and Blaxter (1976) examine the effects that economic constraints have on disabled people endeavouring to live independently. Indeed, Williams (1983) notes that Shearer suggests direct monetary assistance to be the most important resource permitting some people with disabilities to live independently. This has been substantially confirmed by recent studies of the Independent Living Fund, set up specifically to enable disabled people to pay directly for forms of support of their own choosing (Kestenbaum, 1993; Lakey, 1994). There can be no ordinary life and no control over choice or exercise of responsibility in conditions of poverty. In Britain, the level of income maintenance for disabled people is notoriously low, despite recent changes in the benefits system with the introduction of the disability living allowance, which is ostensibly intended to improve the position (Rowlingson and Berthoud, 1994). Arbitrary limits are put on the levels of state support available for people in residential care, unrelated to the actual costs, and, furthermore, the trend in recent years has been for the state to transfer financial responsibility to individuals and their families. Comparison of state retirement pension levels between current and past provision (see Chapter 5), and between Britain and other countries, reveals how far Britain is from guaranteeing those who are not economically active a secure standard of living.

Contrary views

When disabled people read discussions about their position written by people who are not disabled, they respond forcibly. When the first edition of this book was published it provoked strong criticism from disabled writers, notably Jenny Morris (1991). The principal focus of their criticism is that non-disabled commentators write from a viewpoint that, while using them as subjects, excludes disabled people from the analysis. This then leads to a failure to understand disabled people's own perspective. Essentially, their argument is that non-disabled writers see disabled people as a burden and as dependent on society in general and their carers in particular, instead of seeing them as full citizens with the same rights to develop their potential as all other citizens. Rejecting the medical model of disability, which focuses on the extent of their physical or mental impairment, they regard disability as socially defined. While they have impairments that may inhibit their mental or physical functioning, it is society that disables them by refusing to make buildings and transport systems accessible, by excluding people with impairments from employment and by refusing to provide sufficient personal support services for them. They favour the term 'disabled people' because it draws attention to the fact that the disabling comes from society and not from themselves.

Those who adopt this perspective have a particular hostility towards institutional care for disabled people. For them, it represents the way in which society excludes them and herds them together out of sight and out of mind. They believe it emphasizes the model of disability that locates the problem with disabled people themselves – they require full-time care because they cannot look after themselves, they are dependent on others. For the same reason, disabled people have attacked the current emphasis on protecting the interests of carers. Disabled people see an ideological collusion between policy makers and carers, which, again, focuses on the notion of disabled people as dependent, as burdens, as encroaching on the freedom and autonomy of those upon whom they are dependent.

Activists in the disability movement – for example, the British Council of Organisations of Disabled People – campaign powerfully for the right to control their own lives through a variety of strategies. They argue for antidiscrimination legislation (Oliver, 1991; Wood, 1991) as a means of strengthening their position in relation to their participation in the public sphere. They also argue for economic and financial autonomy. Instead of being provided with inadequate services, allocated by uncomprehending professional state employees, disabled people want to receive cash allowances with which to buy the personal assistance they themselves choose. Only in this way, they argue, will they be able to live independent lives – independent in the way *they* define independence (Morris, 1993) – in control of their life circumstances.

In the light of these views, it is hard to present a counterargument. Morris is particularly critical of feminists who try to do so. While she accepts that feminist analysis has an important contribution to make to disability theory – through accepting the personal experience of impairment as a valid component of the disabled person's perspective (rather than focusing on disability as a wholly social creation) (Morris, 1991) – she criticizes feminists for treating 'women' and 'dependent people' (disabled people) as completely separate groups with conflicting interests. This separation extends, in much feminist analysis, she suggests, to working-class women and to black women. It is thus fatally compromised.

When feminists argue for the extension of collectivist principles to the field of care, disabled people find the argument especially hard to accept. For them, even the concept of care is inappropriately applied to their situation. They do not seek care; rather, they require personal assistance or support. Morris calls for the term 'care' to be restored to its rightful mean of caring 'about' and not caring 'for'. They resist the idea that one option might be for personal support to be provided on a collective basis. The memories of institutional care in the past preclude any consideration of new possibilities.

It could be argued, however, that this view is too narrow. There may be circumstances in which collective systems of care are valid, both in terms of basic principles and in relation to the people who might benefit from them. It is significant to note that the priority groups who are the focus of current community care policies are not homogeneous either in type and degree of impairment or, thus, in their need for support. The pertinence of the principles established may vary accordingly. A young person who is physically impaired is in a very different situation from a very elderly person suffering from senile dementia; likewise, a mentally ill, middle-aged individual has different needs and wants from a child who has severe learning difficulties. Young people at the beginning of their lives may be eager to develop social networks; old people facing the end of their lives may be more concerned with consolidating and maintaining existing social networks than seeking new ones. Physical disability requires physical care, especially related to problems of mobility; mental disability requires different forms of supportive care, and chronic sickness may require constant nursing care. These differences have major consequences for the expectations that individuals themselves have of their own lives and for the varieties of care that should be available. Williams (1983) makes a pertinent comment on the heterogeneity of dependency in his critique of the independent living movement in the USA:

> The core constituency of the independent living movement is young, male and 'fit' as opposed to 'frail', whereas a major feature of the social reality of disablement is the elderly female, lacking in robustness and living far from the supportive confines of university campuses [where the independent living movement originated]. It may well be that the disadvantages and needs of an elderly arthritic in an urban slum have more similarity to the problems of her able-bodied neighbours than to the values of the movement for independent living.

There may be a danger, then, if the heterogeneity of dependency is ignored, that certain groups may be excluded from benefiting from developments in patterns of care. In policy and administrative terms, it is relatively straightforward to talk about priority groups as a whole, but the reality of the lives of the people who form those groups is far from straightforward. The flexibility and responsiveness to need, discussed above, has to include the policy and administrative levels, and from there permeate the whole system, involving from the outset the people who are to be in receipt of care (or personal assistance) or their advocates. Indeed, some might argue that only those in receipt of care have any conclusive right to determine types and standards of care. If this is so, the right should also be extended to the other potential partner in the caring dyad – those who provide the care, both paid and unpaid, and who are predominantly women.

A collectivist approach

How might a collectivist approach be best applied to the principles and issues outlined above? First, at the level of principle, collectivism implies a concern felt by members of the group, society or whatever (the collectivity) for other members of the group. This is then translated into responsibility, which is taken up by the collectivity as a whole, with particular subsections or individuals acting as agents for the whole. It is a principle that can at best inspire the group to offer succour and protection to its weakest members, without stigmatizing those in receipt of care. It offers a means of supplying care without dependence on the self-sacrifice that altruistic caring inevitably involves, which in itself then leads to unhealthy relationships of obligation and guilt. It runs directly counter to the principles involved in possessive individualism – the 'charity begins at home' thesis – where self-reliance becomes the dominating virtue that justifies the shutting of doors firmly in the faces of those unable to be self-reliant. According to that view, helping others is a charitable act that enhances the moral worth of the person performing the act and undermines the moral worth of the recipient. Within the collectivist schema, on the other hand, those performing caring tasks and those receiving care are part of a network of reciprocal relationships that binds the whole of society together; the one is at no more of a disadvantage than the other.

At a more practical level, collectivism implies a closer interrelationship between individuals, cross-cutting those other relationships that society typically establishes between people, such as kinship, marriage and occupation. However, these relationships are strong, indeed often overriding, and the task of elevating the collectivist principle to equal them is difficult in a society whose dominant ideology specifically sets out to counter it. In this case, then, how can that dominant ideology be contested, and what strategies can be adopted to ensure that there is an opportunity to introduce the principles of collectivism?

It cannot be a question of standing outside the mainstream of society and hiving off areas of social activity in which to test the principles. Such action would be reminiscent of the utopian experiments of the past or the alternative communities of more recent times. The lessons from them, it should be remembered, are that challenges to current structures must be direct and not oblique. Existing structures must thus be transformed. This may well mean a lack of purity in ideological terms, a making do with what already exists, capitalizing on it and redirecting it towards collectivist goals. Such pragmatic realism should not lose sight of long-term objectives.

These observations may seem high flown, however, when the often unimaginative and pedestrian provision that already exists is examined. The ideals of an integrative, human (and humane), enjoyable and responsive collectivist approach seem far removed, but there are some good as well as poor examples, and it is possible to speculate on the basis of these as to where the future could lie. A number of principles have been outlined so far, which, it is argued, must be observed in any form of care provided for dependent people. They are principles that might pertain to any form of care, so it is important to specify the particular principles and standards to which collective care should be committed; in order to do this, it is necessary to outline the various systems of care envisaged.

The general application of collectivist principles

Most importantly, it means a greater emphasis on *group living* and *group interaction*, especially in contrast to the fragmentation of care and the isolation of both carers and cared for under current community care policies. The benefits of people sharing their everyday experiences (both good and bad), the friendship that this might foster, the help that they can offer each other and the solidarity that may result in the face of adversity should be regarded as positive consequences of collective care. In practical terms, group living might mean small residential units where varying degrees of dependency could be catered for, either with carers living alongside those being cared for or coming in on a regular basis, with dependent people themselves assisting in the care of fellow residents, able-bodied non-carers (in an official, technical sense) living alongside dependent people. In other instances, emphasis may not necessarily be put on the place of residence; it may mean associating as a group on a daily basis, as in the case of day care for children. However, an ethos of group interaction would be fostered, distinguishing it perhaps from many current day care establishments (day hospitals, day centres, luncheon clubs, and so on), where the participants are transported to a central facility on a near-custodial basis and tended in a perfunctory way before being returned home.

A second principle that should be established in any collectivist approach to care is that it should be *shared care*. In cases of heavy dependence, the burden placed on those who provide care is often extreme. Where that burden is unalleviated, where there is no respite, where it is concentrated on too small a resource pool of caring (as it is when a woman alone is expected to care), it becomes intolerably onerous for both carer and cared for alike. As the late Bernard Brett, himself heavily dependent, said:

> Nothing is quite as corrupting for all concerned as being completely dependent on too few people. This also tends to exhaust the helpers, who feel under too much strain, and can lead to the risk of various kinds of abuse. I can promise you, there are few less pleasant things than to be cared for by somebody who is constantly tired and under too much strain. This makes life tense, unpleasant and unfulfilled. (Quoted in Shearer, 1982a, p. 44.)

Morris (1991) points out that Bernard Brett was not advocating residential care as the solution to this problem but arguing strongly for disabled people being able to pay for personal assistance at a level they themselves decide. This does not, however, undermine the point he makes in the excerpt quoted here that relationships between carer and cared for can become unacceptable to both sides if too much is demanded of them.

In collective systems of caring, the burden can be shared and thus the relationship between carer and cared for be neither warped nor corrupted. Because collective living and caring mean the involvement of a stable, mutually known group of individuals, familiarity and continuity become key factors of that care – in contrast to care in the community. Here domiciliary care may be delivered to isolated individuals in their homes by a series of separate professionals, who rarely see each other, have hardly any professional – and certainly no social – contact with each other and who have little time to spend with their patients/clients beyond the strictly measured time it takes to perform the technical caring task. In a collective setting, the fostering of an ethos of sharing care as well as sharing other aspects of communal life is seen as a positive value.

Along with the principle of shared care is one that fosters *group concern* for group members. This is, in a sense, the essential element of collectivism – that which Stedman Jones (1985) argues should underlie any socialist society, but here writ small, relating to the small group of carers and those for whom they are caring. It is perhaps the most difficult to achieve. As Abrams (1977) notes, in relation to what he calls 'neighbourliness', there is a major contradiction between the forces in contemporary society that foster privacy and individualism and assumptions surrounding the concept of 'community spirit', which suggest that there is a fund of common concern and 'neighbourliness' that can be activated to form caring networks. He goes on to argue that, in certain circumstances, this common concern *can* be activated in spite of the ideological contradictions. In the past, it has been through kinship: now he suggests that it is necessary for other institutions – voluntary organizations, statutory services – to take on the activating role. However, there is a great deal of evidence to suggest the contrary in the case of neighbourliness in the community: a number of research studies show that community care in essence means family care and that neighbourliness in that context tends only to be sporadic (Bayley, 1973; Ayer and Alaszewski, 1984; Gilhooly, 1984; Weale, 1990; Donald and Gordon, 1991; Thomas, 1993). Duncan and Hobson (1995), in their right-wing critique of liberal, soft centre-left notions of 'community', draw attention to the failures of current community care in an ironically similar analysis. I would like to argue that it is in the collective setting that that fund of neighbourliness which Abrams refers to might be activated successfully. The enveloping support that collective structures offer might be sufficient to nurture attitudes and responses that are otherwise stifled by the contrary ideological imperatives of individualist society.

This has to happen; collective settings quickly become institution-alized settings if there is no underlying mutual concern felt by those involved. It is this difference in underlying philosophies that differ-entiates the collective setting from the institutional. In physical terms, there may be little difference – numbers of biologically unrelated individuals live together under the same roof, character-ized by some need for care and other support. In one, however, there is a lively integrated community of individuals participating freely and fully in the social life of the group and having relationships with others outside the group, where carers and cared for collaborate. In the other, at worst, there is a collection of separate isolated, often apathetic, individuals warehoused together, serviced by a staff that works in poor and exploiting conditions, having little concern for those in its charge.

A fourth principle that must be incorporated into successful collective settings is the need and the opportunity to develop *ungendered roles*. The uniqueness of the collective setting is that it is different from mainstream economic and social life; because of the extranormal requirement for care, those involved do not *routinely* have to follow the norms and expectations that wider society impresses on its other members. The young mother who is bedbound does not 'automatically' expect to take up a domestic role *vis-à-vis* housework and childrearing as she would (because of normative attitudes at large) if she were able-bodied. Others will perform that role, and in a collective setting they may be men or women, able-bodied or at least more so than she. Living in a collec-tive setting, she will have far more options available than if she were restricted to getting by with domiciliary care provided in her own nuclear family home, with the man going out to work in the 'normal' way. Her chance of greater contact with both children and friends is more likely, as is the opportunity to find a constructive role in the life of the community, than if she were shut up in her small house alone all day. Similarly, the man with greatly restricted mobility will not necessarily expect to go out to work to support his family in the traditional way; he might take on a 'domestic' role in the collective setting. The division of labour by gender based on notions such as physical strength and mental superiority is suddenly revealed as redundant in settings where these notions have little meaning. Individuals contribute whatever skills they are able to, regardless of age or gender.

In the case of children, be they able-bodied or mentally or physically impaired, the possibilities are just as great. The occasion of their dependency gives rise in the collective setting to the opportunity of breaking through the stereotyped roles generally foisted on them. Whatever the condition of their dependency, whether they are in full-time residential care or day care, the opportunity is there for a casting off of gendered approaches to care. As things stand at present though, when a child becomes the responsibility of the state, the usual response is to place him or her in a foster or adoptive family, where the opportunity will be lost. Families are often chosen specifically for the stability of their nuclear relationships – the closer to the model a family approximates, the greater the likelihood will be that they will be chosen as prospective parents, and the greater the likelihood of their assuming stereotyped gendered attitudes and roles. (There tends to be a hierarchy of fosterability. Thus children without impairments are expected to go into 'model' families, while in the case of children with severe impairments, the norm is far less rigorously applied, so that single parents or single people are welcomed.)

The particular case of child care

The question of children is crucial: the collective alternative should not be seen simply as a solution to the problems of old age and adult dependency. By ensuring that collective approaches to childcare become acceptable in an everyday sense – through afterschool play schemes (as opposed to childminders, au pairs or the latch key) and day nurseries for preschool children (as opposed to nannies, childminders, playgroups plus mother, mothers at home all day) – it becomes a mainstream concept that does not stand out as remarkable, and thus unacceptable, when applied to the issue of adult care.

The view that childcare is best performed collectively has been widely accepted by the women's movement during the past twenty years. Research has contested the findings of Bowlby and his followers and has demonstrated cogently the feasibility of alternative approaches (New and David, 1985). Thus it is now possible to argue in a scientifically respectable, as well as a 'merely' polemical, fashion that children benefit from being brought up in the company of other children, that they relate happily to more adults than their mothers and other biologically related individuals, and that they do not suffer irreparable damage if separated from their mothers for social activities at a very young age. So the everyday business of childcare could well be collectivized, resulting in a decrease in the number of women isolated at home and a decrease in the number of children cared for by individual surrogate mothers – be they childminders, nannies or au pairs. Collective forms of childcare could be run in a variety of ways by a variety of agencies: local authorities could extend their facilities as part of their general children's services – schools, libraries, leisure and recreation services – rather than simply as part of social services provision as at present, which tends to foster the stigmatized image of children's day care as only being available for children from 'problem families'. Local communities could provide neighbourhood schemes; workplace nurseries could be organized. More informal arrangements could be set up between groups of friends and neighbours. New and David (1985) provide a comprehensive and critical assessment of this variety of options.

There are, of course, many countries in Europe where such collective provision is the norm. In many cases, women have good maternity leave provision that includes transferable maternity pay and access to good nursery facilities, which provide comprehensive, secure and stimulating care in environments that foster group activity and group consciousness. Starting from such an inclusive basis, it would be possible to develop ungendered forms of play and social activity that would stimulate social interaction in later life – if the will were there. As we noted in earlier chapters, collectivism does not automatically mean feminism; that has to be consciously incorporated.

As collective childcare came to be seen as positively beneficial for all sorts of children, the need to introduce separate forms of provision for disabled children would diminish. Disability in whatever form differentiates and separates children from each other to a much lesser extent the younger the children are. If it became usual for all preschool children to go to nursery, a community of local children would develop in preschool years that would continue into school, and problems of integration and/or segregation once school age had been reached would be resolved. Services for special needs could be introduced into that community of children for those who needed them as and when appropriate; labelling of children as either able-bodied or disabled in order to satisfy administratively defined criteria might thus be avoided.

Where highly specialized services were necessary, the underlying philosophy of group concern and group support, which is part of the collectivist approach, should allow for the development of communal residential facilities that were not 'bins' or 'warehouses' but positive exercises in shared living. The argument against such provision is the argument over integration as opposed to segregation – that by hiving off those who are dependent from mainstream society, society is condemning them to a life of disadvantage, as oddities, different from the rest of society. Jones (1972) suggests that the term 'segregation' is used to describe something that is intrinsically damaging and unacceptable. The use of the term 'specialization', however, does not carry the same connotation and might usefully be applied to certain forms of care or treatment (she cites the setting up of specialist services for dyslexic children). Living in communal groups might be seen by some as a form of segregated living, but it might also be seen as an expression of specialist concern for those living in the groups. The parents quoted in the Select Committee report (House of Commons, 1985) who favour communal provision for their disabled children certainly feel that way. There has been a continuing difference of view expressed between some pressure groups acting on behalf of people with learning difficulties and the families of those people about the appropriateness of special villages catering specifically for them. A group called Rescare argued very powerfully in 1995 for maintaining such provision, while VIA (Values into Action, previously the Campaign for Mentally Handicapped People) has contested this strongly. The difference of opinion reflects the contrasting philosophies that such groups have adopted. Rescare argues that villages can offer humane, individualized care while at the same time providing security and companionship; contact with the surrounding community is valued (Cox and Pearson, 1995). VIA, on the other hand, believes that such communities deny the people living there the opportunity to exercise choice or to participate fully in wider society (Collins, 1995). It believes, perhaps uncritically, that resettlement in small houses in ordinary streets offers both, although there is evidence to suggest that it does not (Wing, 1990).

There are already initiatives in group living that measure up to some of the objectives outlined above. In the residential care sector, those who are conscious of the failures of familial-based policies and who perceive the benefits of the collective approach to care are working hard to bring them to fruition. Keith White (1986), for example, himself involved in such an approach at Mill Grove – argues precisely along these lines. First he questions the pre-eminent value placed on the family model of care:

> What do we mean by the 'family experience', for example, that is so vital for a child that any number of placements will be risked to attain it.

He goes on to posit the communal alternative, in which:

> the combination of a shared space, or place, and people committed to living and sharing together, produces a significant force or pressure towards integrating the life and daily work of the community. It is partly to do with the scale of the enterprise, partly to do with a desire to avoid splitting off specialist tasks and functions. The divisions to which we have become so accustomed in twentieth century urban living between art and science, work and family, consumption and production, education and leisure, feelings and mind, management and work-force, public and private, are challenged.

There are many other examples of innovative approaches to the integration of caring and group living, mostly, it should be said, in the voluntary sector; local authority homes based on other principles have rarely matched them. Indeed, one of the distressing developments in recent years has been the revelations of extensive abuse that has taken place in children's homes over the years. Yet there have been occasions on which children in children's homes have grouped together to defend their way of life, arguing that they prefer to live together rather than be dispersed to individual, separate foster families. In the 1980s, young people in England themselves formed an association (National Association of Young People in Care), which, amongst other things, advised children on how to counter legal moves to close their homes; in several cases, children succeeded in blocking such moves (*Community Care*, 1984).

Of course, there may well be numbers of young adults who are disabled who simply wish to 'normalise' (Wolfensberger, 1972, 1983; Brown and Smith, 1992) their living circumstances according to the accepted roles and attitudes current in contemporary society – that is, gendered and individualist. They must have the freedom to do so, although the concept of living independently often means the wish simply to escape from the constraints of dependency on their nuclear family of birth. One way of doing this is to live collectively with people of their own choice.

To return to the question of caring for older people, the issue of living independently – as Williams (1983) points out – is less relevant. They often have no close relatives – they *are* living on their own, but often isolated and lonely, with few choices open to them. One of the few options open to them, and only *in extremis*, will be a move into residential or institutional care as their dependency increases. Thus it is important that such care is of high quality and the right sort. There is no reason why collective care should not be provided that improves the quality of old people's lives, in terms of personal relationships and companionship, concerned care and comfort and a feeling that their lives are still worth living.

It does not tend to be seen like that, however. Residential provision is disliked by policy makers, practitioners and some elderly people because much existing provision is seen to be (or believed to be) the outcome of an underlying custodial philosophy, which seeks to cut people off from existing social networks without thought for individual needs. Collective provision could just as easily be structured on the premise that it might suit the needs and inclinations of elderly people. There is much evidence to the contrary (for example Townsend, 1962; Booth, 1985), but indications from further afield show that there *are* forms of collective provision that elderly people find acceptable. These will be considered next.

Examples of collective living schemes

In Scandinavia and the Netherlands, for example, collective provision seems to be generally acceptable even where establishments are extremely large (Pearson, 1982). Sheltered housing, communally shared facilities and access to integral nursing home accommodation, together with the daily participation of other elderly people from the surrounding locality, all seem to be the norm for those needing some form of care. Denmark seems to have the most highly developed and comprehensive schemes. Young (1985) describes those where there is sheltered accommodation with highly accessible toilet facilities (important in maintaining independence), communal dining rooms, lounges and recreation rooms, with laundries, hairdressing, libraries, and occupational therapy all available, and where there is nursing home accommodation within the same complex (which avoids some of the problems associated with moving people along a continuum of care).

Other large-scale schemes have more complex facilities, involving sheltered flats, 'day homes' to cater for medically referred people and 'day centres', along with nursing homes for residents to use when required, and the usual communal servicing and social facilities, including dining rooms and kitchens available to non-resident local pensioners. Some of them may cater for large numbers of people (three hundred residents and up to four hundred daily visitors), and there is a degree of dispute as to what might be the optimum size (Bertolt and Bertolt, 1983). However, surveys of residents and applicants for places indicate general satisfaction. One study, for example, cites 69 per cent as approving the multifunctional centre plus nursing home facilities, with 88 per cent expressing satisfaction with a good level of social contacts. Only 30 per cent express any support for the idea of integration with other age groups, 'inter-generational' living, with only 20 per cent of those who have already experienced it supporting it (Ensomme Gamles Vaern, 1980). Thus the arguments about segregation/specialization as opposed to integration are not easily resolved. This is mirrored in the findings of a study of sheltered housing in Britain, where only 4 per cent wished to live in settings with children as neighbours, while 37 per cent opted to live in settings exclusively inhabited by other elderly people (Butler *et al.*, 1983). Barr (1977) reports high levels of satisfaction with single-generation living in the USA (78 per cent in this case).

Other reports from the USA confirm the positive attitudes to collective forms of living – or 'shared care' (Streib *et al.*, 1984). They argue cogently in favour of this arrangement for the elderly, which ranges from individual elderly people sharing their own homes with another individual to residential settings where groups of elderly people live in the same house, sometimes with resident staff, sometimes with staff coming in on a daily basis. In a survey of shared living arrangements in the USA with reference also to Britain and Sweden, they take account of well-known views that are hostile to the shared living, or residential, option for the elderly. These, they recognize, suggest that 'age-dense' environments lead to the ghettoiza-tion of the elderly into what old age advocate Maggie Kuhn called 'geriatric playpens'. However, they cite a number of studies that conclude that many elderly people *prefer* living in age-concentrated settings, leading to enhanced morale, 'life satisfaction' and a decrease in 'disengagement from social interaction'. While they recognize that professionals and elderly people themselves may have varied opinions about what constitutes acceptable provision, they stress that it is important that the option should be there for those who choose it; the shared living option is as intrinsically valid as others that are frequently suggested. They note its positive benefits as compared to some of the 'disbenefits' of living at home alone:

> Those who advocate keeping the elderly in their homes as long as possible do not address the fact that when an increasing array of services are supplied, the elderly may gradually assume the social role of 'recipients' – persons to whom much is given and from whom nothing is expected – a dependent role that has only rights and no duties. In shared living arrangements, the residents have informal social roles. They must get up in the morning, get dressed, come to meals, and interact with other family [that is, those sharing the communal facilities], and they are expected to participate in at least some of the family activities… In short, the normative expectations are those of *participation*. Shared living keeps an older person's interaction mechanisms intact, and he or she is not as likely to withdraw. We have been informed of residents who were withdrawn and depressed, absorbed in their own misery, but, after a few weeks of shared living, began to relate to other people in the home and take an interest in their surroundings and in the ongoing parade of life. (Streib *et al.*, 1984, p. 216)

They utilize Kahn and Antonucci's (1981) concept of the 'convoy' – that subset of people upon whom a person relies and, in turn, the set of people who rely upon that individual for support through the processes of the lifecycle, suggesting that when former networks and support systems (the convoy) diminish (through death, illness, isolation, retirement, and so on), a shared living group might take on the role of the new 'convoy'. Streib *et al.* suggest that this approach is confirmed by findings from studies that they review.

Additional evidence from the USA suggests that there is also enthusiasm for other forms of collective living. There are several descriptions of retirement villages, purpose-built to house elderly people, with communal service facilities and leisure activities provided on a comprehensive scale, together with nursing care where necessary. Torres and Trotzky (1982) describe what are called 'life care' communities – residential village communities, in this case organized on a non-profit, non-sectarian basis (set up by their founders as part of a 'commitment to social justice'), providing 200 living units with a 60-bed skilled nursing care unit set in large grounds of more than 20 acres. Other retirement communities have been set up with profit in mind, but the aim, apparently, is the same – to provide comprehensive, specialist (or segregated) collective facilities for the elderly to cover all aspects of daily living, including care, nursing care and medical care when necessary. Sun City is perhaps one of the most well-known enterprises and has been written about and shown on television in Britain. Here a whole town has been built for elderly people, and the emphasis has been placed on active participation. Thus the elderly residents themselves provide and staff the police force, the litter collection unit, the hospital and library facilities and all manner of other municipal functions (Dearman, 1982).

In the Netherlands, communal living has become increasingly popular over the years. In part, this may be accounted for by a traditional expectation on the part of most retired people of moving into some form of residential care as they get older. However, communal care is represented as something different: an active approach to ageing, with positive value placed on the benefits of shared living, as innovative and as independent from the mainstream residential system (Baars and Thomese, 1994). The authors report that five per cent of older people in the Netherlands live in some form of communal living arrangement, which is the equivalent, in some countries, of the total number of people living in residential care of all types.

Even in Britain there are signs that older people are deciding for themselves that more imaginative approaches than exist at present might be appropriate, although sheltered housing tends to be the preferred option of a majority of people, in spite of drawbacks about moving on in times of heavy dependency and the problematic functions of the wardens in such schemes (Butler *et al.*, 1983). Housing Associations such as Anchor and Hanover have expanded substantially over the past ten years, adding extra care services to residents as part of the package in some schemes. A number of companies have entered the retirement home business, building retirement apartments for sale for those older people with capital. An increasing number of pensioners are taking up package holidays to the sun (mostly to Spain), often spending the winter months at cut-price rates in hotels glad of the trade in otherwise empty months (Whitehouse, 1984). Communal activities and social networks in these settings are developed in a way in which planners of services for older people might only envy, and it is successful solely because it stems from older people's own inclinations and ideas. However, it costs money: pensioners have to be able to afford even the cut-rate prices on offer. The companies running the packages are in it for profit. In another context, private old people's homes, residential homes and nursing homes have always been chosen by the well-heeled middle classes as they decline into dependency, as noted by Aneurin Bevan during the period of the 1945 Labour Government in Britain (Means and Smith, 1983). The stigma so often associated with public provision of the same type is absent in these cases, which may say something about the way in which class, cash and antistate rhetoric impinge on the formation of attitudes to welfare.

It is important at this point to consider the substantial growth in residential and nursing home care in Britain since the beginning of the 1980s – just at the time when central government was promoting its community care policies. Between 1981 and 1991, the number of people in residential homes and hostels, for example, increased by two fifths (Central Statistical Office, 1995, Table 8.21). Most of this growth took place within the private sector. Indeed, as has been noted earlier, the NHS has been withdrawing from the provision of long-term care in recent years; similarly, local authorities have been turning over their residential homes to private or charitable control as a result of recent community care legislation. Notwithstanding the reluctance on the part of government to support it, people have nevertheless been choosing to adopt the residential option. There are different views on why this should be so. It is commonly argued that the perverse incentives offered by the social security system during the 1980s, which allowed people to claim substantial payments to cover the cost of residential care even though official policy was to promote community care, was one reason. Others have argued that people were 'forced' into residential care during the period because there were no alternatives – community care services were too underdeveloped. No-one has suggested (even in this period of consumer sovereignty) that it was because older people themselves wanted to take up the option. There are grounds for suggesting that some useful research might be conducted into older people's preferences in relation to living options that was not constrained by the policy fashion of the day.

Even in the inhospitable policy climate of Britain during the 1980s and 90s, and even with recent changes in social security that have closed the loophole mentioned above, a variety of residential forms of living arrangements has developed with some form of communal ethos involved. Perhaps the best example is of the Abbeyfield Society, which was established in the 1950s but has grown significantly in recent years. Its chief aim from the outset was to provide communal living for older people that would combat the loneliness and isolation that it recognized even then threatened the lives of many retired people. The Society runs a range of residential homes where small groups of older people share accommodation within a stated ethos of collective support. In recent years, 'extra care' has also been provided to support residents as they become more infirm (Abbeyfield Society, 1989).

Housing Associations are probably showing some of the most imaginative approaches to developing collective living arrangements for older people. The Anchor and Hanover associations have grown from simple providers of sheltered housing to organizations that seek to offer a comprehensive system of care and support for a range of older people with a variety of needs. However, these are two of many. It is perhaps ironic that it should be the private and not-for-profit sectors that have been developing the most imaginative approaches to collective forms of living rather than the state, which might have been expected to bear the responsibility of caring for its older and more vulnerable citizens.

As well as catering for the needs of older people, communal forms have found favour in other situations. In the field of mental illness, the therapeutic community is an accepted means of providing care and support (Jansen, 1980). The Richmond Fellowship runs many such communities to support young people suffering from schizophrenia, for example. The concept of the therapeutic community places emphasis on the integration of all members of the group–staff and patients alike – consciously underplaying the division between experts (staff) and non-experts (patients). It values members for themselves and not for skills they may or may not have to offer. It stresses the 'communalism' that Maxwell Jones, a pioneer in the field who established communities in hospitals first at Belmont and then at Dingleton, favoured. Others, too, have stressed the value of 'asylum' for people with mental health problems; they argue the importance of retreats being made available for people in crisis (Laing, 1985). The Camphill village communities for people with learning difficulties are other examples of the benefits of communal living. The refuges set up by Women's Aid during the 1970s for women battered by their menfolk also offered and continue to offer collective solutions, in this case to the problems of fear and of enforced homelessness.

Public, voluntary or private provision

The collective living schemes referred to in this chapter represent a mix of public, voluntary and private provision. That mix, however, has undergone profound changes in Britain in recent years. Private residential care has burgeoned over the past ten years, while local authority care has shrunk. As noted earlier, the private sector grew rapidly in the 1980s largely as a result of social security arrangements that unintentionally favoured people choosing to go into residential or nursing home care. As a result of the NHS and community care reforms enacted in 1990, local authority provision began to be scaled down. One of the main aims of the reforms was to favour the 'mixed economy of welfare', and local authorities were required to spend a substantial part of the community care funding, which they became responsible for, directly in the private sector (McGlone and Cronin, 1994). One of the immediate effects was that local authorities began to close down their own provision or to transfer or transform it into not-for-profit independent organizations.

The argument about the relative merits of private, statutory and voluntary provision have been overtaken in recent years, directly as a consequence of these developments. Care provided by the state has to a large degree become residual, often acting as a fall-back or safety net. Questions about quality and standards of care arise in such situations; too often, state-provided care will be seen as second best – and turn out to be second best – but, of course, private care is not always good. Private care for older people has become big business in both Britain and the USA, and concern has been expressed about its adequacy – witness the revelations published by Vladeck (1980) in the USA and the passing of the Registered Homes Act in 1984 in Britain, which attempted to regulate the quality of residential and nursing home care in Britain.

After 1979 and the moving of general debate to the right, it has become commonplace to argue the case for welfare pluralism: that the state cannot and should not provide care and treatment in all cases, and that the private and voluntary sectors have a place within the general schema of welfare. In reality, it is not a straight fight between private and state provision of welfare – the role of the voluntary sector is also involved, often as exemplar. Because it operates outside the constraints of statutory duties on the one hand, and not for profit on the other, and perhaps because it is not staffed exclusively by professionals fixed in their practice by the ideologies and cultures of their particular professions, the voluntary sector may be able to introduce radical ideas and new ways of organizing. The Richmond Fellowship and Women's Aid have already been mentioned, but there are numerous other examples, ranging from self-help groups concerned with particular disabling conditions, to activists' groups and pressure groups such as Citizen Advocacy groups (Dunning, 1995) and SANE (for people with schizophrenia and their families). However, it can be argued that the position of the voluntary sector has been compromised with the introduction of the internal market under the 1990 reforms. How far it is able to retain its stance as an innovator in the face of demands to become involved in the contracting culture of the internal market remains to be seen. The fear is that because voluntary organizations will be drawn into tightly drawn contracts and service level agreements with purchasers (local or health authorities), there will be fewer opportunities for experimenting with new ideas. It has long been recognized that the voluntary sector can sometimes best express the authentic view of dependent people themselves and can most readily test out new ideas in policy and practice. It will be an unfortunate and unforeseen consequence of the reforms if this ceases to be the case.

The role of the voluntary sector could be crucial in the introduction and development of the collectivist, feminist principles that might underpin new approaches to caring. So far it has been demonstrated that systems of care provision already exist that go some way along the road to collective care. It is possible, so the evidence shows, to organize collective provision – be it in small, ordinary houses, hostels and other intermediate forms, or even on a large 'age-dense' scale – *and* for it to be acceptable to those for whom it is intended.

However, much of it does not address the twin issues of equitable access and non-sexist philosophies and structures.

On the first count, whether there is appropriate provision available or not depends, at the moment, largely on the vagaries of a mix of idiosyncratic voluntary sector provision and the statutory services (both of which tend to operate in a mutual policy and planning vacuum), and on the ability to pay for such services. Neither barrier is acceptable. On the second count, there is an almost total absence of non-sexist options. Few, if any, communal initiatives in the field of care provision operate on explicitly stated feminist principles, and it is unlikely that any of them incorporate such principles in an unarticulated way. In a culture that generally sets its face against the feminist position, it is almost impossible for structures within it to operate on an *implicitly* feminist basis. Oppositional approaches, precisely because they are oppositional, can only progress by being *explicit* – by 'standing up and being counted'. It is perhaps the voluntary sector, on a slow and perhaps piecemeal basis, that can first make these approaches explicit. While purists might say that society as a whole must take collective responsibility for the provision of care in every instance, it would be more realistic and practical to seize on every opportunity as it arises to test out the claims of collectivism, thereby demonstrating their worth.

Low pay, low status: the rewards of caring

There is a further issue of immense importance. Those providing care within existing residential establishments are mostly women, and, by and large, they are low paid and of low status. In any reconsideration of existing structures and efforts to introduce new approaches, the position of women as workers and carers has to be taken into account. It was pointed out earlier that employment for women in the public sector tends to replicate their domestic functions; they are concentrated into low-status caring occupations and are poorly paid. If one of the aims of introducing new forms of collective care is to remove the arbitrary burden placed upon women who have to care informally, this of necessity means that there are likely to be many more paid posts in the formal caring sector. It is of paramount importance that these new jobs and the new structures within which they are located do not simply mimic existing structures and existing working terms and conditions.

It is a central tenet of the feminist view of the world that such work is not intrinsically of low worth, just as women, intrinsically, do not constitute a lower order than men. The low value of women and the low value attached to their work, and the caring role in particular, mutually reinforce each other because they are divested of power – a power that tends to be *in*vested in men and that attaches to the roles men perform. It is essentially a question of inequality; until that issue is generally confronted, the imbalance as it relates to work in the public sphere can never be redressed. Over the past ten years, particularly through the recession of the late 1980s and early 1990s, unemployment increased and a downward pressure on wages was exerted. Inevitably, those working in the low-paid care sector suffered the repercussions.

However, there are other reasons why caring tends to remain low paid. First, women themselves, for reasons discussed in an earlier chapter, tend to accept the *status quo* and do not make radical demands for reassessment of their working roles. Second, the chronic shortage of resources imposes constraints on the introduction of policy change, which might have resource implications. Third, there is a hierarchy of professional interest involved in the provision of many of the services in question. The women who perform the physical, caring tasks – hospital and community nurses, care attendants, nursing auxiliaries, home care workers – are at the bottom of this hierarchy. To alter their status would have repercussions on that constellation of professions that presently has superior status – social workers, doctors, managers and administrators – and one of the features of these professions (at least at their senior levels) is that they tend to be predominantly male.

Sources have drawn attention to the manner in which the profession of social work has changed over the years. From being the preserve of charitably minded and middle-class women, it has become a predominantly male-managed profession, careful to delineate and jealously guard its boundaries, ensuring that social workers do not perform any task (be it welfare rights advice or cleaning a dirty house) outside those boundaries – which would otherwise demean them – and at the same time preventing any other profession encroaching upon their self-defined territory. Davis and Brook quote some telling examples of the male takeover of social work as a profession. They cite Malcolm Wicks as saying:

To care for the children 'in care' in the sixties, we do not seek only the warm motherly type, filled with emotional 'gush' for the 'poor dear children', we seek humane, gay, tolerant, sensible men and women of good intelligence, who can have their natural abilities trained to do therapeutic work with hard, bitter, aggressive, vulgar and unappreciative children. The kind of men and women we need with the ambition to do worthwhile work on behalf of the community are available but the image of the house-parent, as a glorified domestic or a warm, buxom, motherly type is repellent to them and often they seek to achieve their ambitions and satisfy their vocations in other ways. (Davis and Brook, 1985, p. 21)

They comment:

Wicks was contrasting what he clearly thought were male and female styles of care – to the detriment of the female. Women were amateur and emotional in their approach to child care. To be professional depended on a partnership between men and women. This was not all; the basis of that partnership had a familiar ring, in that it mirrored the relationship between men and women that was an intrinsic part of family life. (Davis and Brook, 1985, p. 21)

Finch and Groves, in the same contributed volume, go on to warn of the implications for women of the current interest, within social work, in community social work and some forms of patch-based service delivery:

Under the patch-based system teams of social work assistants, paid volunteers, and unpaid carers operate in small geographical areas under the supervision of a professional social worker who interweaves social work and the community. The system appears to involve an upwardly mobile and career-oriented male patch-leader with a train of female patchworkers (alias social work assistants, home helps and wardens). (Finch and Groves, 1985, p. 103)

Men have captured the heights and will be loth to relinquish them. Even if the issue of gendered domination is set aside, sociological study of the professions demonstrates that professions (however defined) jealously protect their strategic interests – boundaries, conditions, training and remuneration all being central. They may not take kindly to a reassessment of professional status that a revaluing of the caring role and of those who perform it would entail. So it will be a long haul. That there has to be such a reassessment and revaluation, if collective forms of care are to be regarded by feminists as acceptable, is essential, but there are problems even so. There may be a danger that raising the issue of wages and working conditions as part of the process of revaluation may alter the relationship between carers and cared for to the detriment of the latter, introducing what Peace (1984) calls 'the bureaucratic dimension' at the cost of affective (seen by her as 'familial') aspects. She argues that the personalized, informal concern that carers typically develop for those whom they are tending would be pushed aside by a self-interested concern for status, job remit and wage rates. She bases this view on two fundamental assumptions: first, that there are two opposed modes of caring – the bureaucratic and the affective – which are mutually exclusive, and second, that in introducing industrial relations concepts, relating to terms and conditions, into the formal caring relationship automatically means opting for the bureaucratic rather than the affective mode. Closely linked to this view is one that believes that the best way to provide formal care is to mimic *in*formal family care (and that this means the affective mode). Thus Cunnison (1984) quotes Heumann and Boldy's description of the sheltered housing warden as 'a paid family proxy', where 'the warden's home is her place of work, and the residents her extended family'. This view, she concludes succinctly, is romanticized.

Feminists have to ask whether indeed the bureaucratic/affective dichotomy exists, and if so, whether it is causally linked to the manner in which carers are employed. It brings directly into focus the ideological premises upon which attitudes to forms of care are based. For those who see formal care as second best, its most acceptable form is that based on the family model of care. This presumes women's altruism and has a vested interest in playing down any interest in formal terms and conditions of the carers' employment. To allow such interest to develop would, according to this view, allow bureaucratic attitudes to care to become established. There is, however, a contrary view, one that feminists would agree with: that the affective, if it means familial, almost *implies* the bureaucratic wherever formal caring is concerned. Cunnison (1984, p. 122), for instance, recognizes that under the present system there is a 'tension between humanitarian values and the sale of labour power which underlies many of their (the sheltered housing wardens) problems'.

Under such a system, women who work as carers in the formal sense are confronted by the contradiction between the expectations of their altruism, on the one hand, and the harsh realities of overwork and underpay, on the other. Cunnison describes how wardens cope with this in one of three ways: by accepting the dominant view of their expected altruism and making the best of a bad job; by withdrawal, through resignation or falling into mental or physical illness; or by compromise – by sticking to the letter of the job description at the cost of their affective relationship with their tenants. Thus the affective relationship is penetrated by the bureaucratic and vice versa – which is clearly unacceptable.

In a better world, such choices would be unnecessary. There is no intrinsic reason why humane care has to be provided by low-status, low-paid carers, and there is no intrinsic reason why humane care has to be modelled on family-based forms (which may not necessarily be humane anyway). 'Humane' does not have to mean 'altruistic', and 'affective' does not have to mean 'familial'. For example, in the predominantly male world of general medical practice, these issues simply do not arise. Concern for those whom GPs care for in no way excludes an overriding interest in the terms and conditions of their contracts: the British Medical Association has always fought powerfully for improved conditions of service for its members. General medical practitioners would argue that they can only provide a satisfactory 'caring service' if they are well paid and the conditions in which they work are of adequate standard. This ability to maintain concern for their patients and a lively concern for their pockets is clearly linked to the high position of the status that doctors occupy in the professional hierarchy and the fact that it is (still) a predominantly male profession, at least in the higher reaches. They are able to call the tune and establish the ground rules in their own interests.

This much is certain then: the familial model of care that currently dominates is based on premises that are unacceptable to feminists and (often) to those who are themselves dependent on care. I have suggested that there are alternative, collective approaches to care that ought to be considered and which can capitalize on structures that in fact already exist. As we have seen, the collectivist philosophy has been a continuing theme in welfare provision over the centuries. The question posed here is, why not build on that underlying current and transform existing attitudes and expectations? However, in doing so, certain principles must be observed. The rights and expectations of disabled and other dependent people themselves must be guaranteed, along with the rights and expectations of those (predominantly women, but perhaps in the future both men and women) who provide the care in the formal, public sector.

7

The future for collectivism

Throughout this book, I have tried to argue that the intimate business of caring for chronically dependent people is directly linked to the wider responsibility that society, as a whole, has for all its members; the small-scale concerns of individuals in the caring sphere form part of the wider concerns of society at large. Thus the manner in which individuals care for each other is not simply a matter of personal and practical response to particular needs: it is permeated by the ideological attitudes upon which other social relations are also based.

In earlier chapters, we examined some of those attitudes, and it was suggested that the ideology of familism and the philosophy of possessive individualism dominate the conceptual frameworks of contemporary Western society. Social structure and its related pattern of social relations are underpinned by this ideological base. It is this ideology of familism that links the individual's circumstances of caring with society's organization of welfare. The familial model of care, encouraged and depended upon at the level of the individual, becomes the model for social provision as a whole.

Moreover, this dominant ideology of familism and possessive individualism has been in continuous competition with a contradictory impulse, namely the pull towards collectivism. English society and that of other parts of north-west Europe over the centuries have been characterized as highly individualistic, yet at the same time have displayed a deep-seated recognition of the need to take a collective responsibility for their weaker members. The strength of that recognition has varied over time – the late nineteenth century was a period when the virtues of self-reliance were preached. Likewise the

151

apparent ascendancy of the new right during the 1980s seemed to challenge the assumption that society has an obligation to take on that responsibility. Nevertheless, the impulse is there, and I have tried to argue the case for building on it.

Collectivism, however, is a concept of several parts. Collectivist ideology as it relates to the broad issues of responsibility for care and welfare in society occupies a long-held and honourable position in Western culture. However, as it relates to the private (domestic) domain and especially when it involves collective *forms* as well, it becomes a much more contested concept, disputed not only by anticollectivists, but also by those supporting the collectivist principle in its broadest sense. Collectivists of this latter sort tend to want to exclude it from the domestic domain, keeping that private and 'familized'. However, there is plenty of evidence to show that this conscious exclusion is not universal; there are cultures and there have been times when collectivist principles have penetrated deep into the domestic domain.

The need for change in personal, public and official attitudes

It is on the basis of this knowledge that feminists hold that their belief in the widest possible application of collectivist principles is feasible. Thus they seek to argue the case for extending the collective basis of welfare (specifically as it relates to the provision of care), allying it with the basic feminist principle of non-gendered action. They have no difficulty in maintaining that their case is both sound and plausible. They recognize that the tasks that are traditionally allocated to women are tasks that are essential, in the most basic terms, to survival – that is, after all, what reproduction is about. Social reproduction is essentially the continuance of those who are alive, from day to day; thus it involves the servicing, maintenance and succouring of social actors. And, of course, biological reproduction is ensuring that one generation of those social actors is succeeded by another.

Feminists obviously recognize the necessity of both these functions but object to the way in which they have been relegated to the private, domestic sphere, with women confined along with them. Domestic labour has been both the means and the symbol of women's subordination. However, they do not argue that the central tasks of domestic labour can be abolished. The solution is twofold. First, domestic labour should not be performed by women only; there is no intrinsic reason why men and women cannot both undertake it. Second, the domestic, private sphere should be opened up. The division of labour within the nuclear family should be broken down, and the major tasks of the domestic sphere should be shared or collectivized, those major tasks being defined as childcare, the care of other dependent people and, perhaps, the preparation and allocation of food. Other tasks may be better 'individualized' rather than collectivized – there is no reason why a woman should clean up or wash clothes for other people in today's machine-rich age. Most adults are able to press buttons and therefore maintain themselves, especially if they live in collective settings where machines and other facilities are more likely to be available. Technological advances in other spheres (our lives having been transformed by computers and microtechnology in so many areas) should be matched within the domestic sphere. Much has been written by feminists on the need to reorganize personal life; less has been written about collectivist approaches to other areas of social life that would thus cease to be relegated to, or isolated in, the domestic sphere, especially in relation to the caring function. It has been the purpose of this text to explore some of the alternatives that might be involved.

It is by opening up the domestic sphere and introducing collectivist principles into the hearth of familism that the strength of that ideology can be challenged. Feminists have long argued that the personal is political; thus the act of questioning and changing some of the assumptions upon which the business of daily living and caring is based will have profound repercussions at other levels of society. It is because of this that I have argued that to change current approaches in childcare – from the individualist mode to the collectivist – can influence approaches to other sorts of care. First, it would open up ways of thinking about the care of disabled children and the care of children 'in care'. Thence it would affect the way we think about caring for a whole range of other individuals, notably those who are very dependent, particularly infirm and confused older people.

However, change at the personal level, at the domestic level, is not enough. Changes in wider attitudes have to take place; indeed, without them changes at the domestic level would be slow to emerge. This circular relationship – of change at the personal level being dependent on society-wide change in 'public' attitudes, which in turn are dependent on the receptivity and willingness of individuals to change their personal attitudes – is one of the key problems in understanding how ideological attitudes are both formed and are open to change. It may be something to do with the conjuncture of particular sets of factors at particular periods of time. Thus it will not be the single factor of demographic change, of the growth of a socio-political movement, of charismatic intellectual leadership or of economic pressure that will effect change on its own. It will be more to do with a series of these single factors coinciding and coalescing to alter the 'climate of the times'.

Of course, there have to be changes not only in personal and public attitudes, but also at the political and professional levels. Attitudinal change has to be incorporated into the 'official discourse' of policy makers and practitioners. The state welfare complex, controlled by the political bureaucracy and staffed by members of the professions, performs a central role in the provision of care. It is crucial, then, that changes in attitudes penetrate that sphere too. The 'caring professions' are perhaps central in this; their current advocacy of the familial model of care has played a key part in its becoming accepted as the dominant model. However, the 'caring professions' are not a uniform body; there have been, and remain, sharp differences in attitudes and perceptions about the issue of caring amongst this variety of occupations.

The strength of professional definitions of dependency

The medical model of health and illness that has dominated much of the thinking of the health professions (doctors and nurses in particular) over the past hundred years, and which tends to see ill-health as disease-centred, individualized and responsive to medicotechnical intervention, has tended to promote the development of all that is worst in the institutionalized care of dependent people. The history of caring for mentally ill people is a good example. Manning and Oliver (1985) note that control of 'the mad' during the nineteenth century came firmly under medical direction within the large asylums that characterized the period. In fact, they seem to suggest that medical control was something of a 'putsch', taking over from the 'moral treatment' that had accompanied the introduction of the asylums in the early nineteenth century and that had been in the hands of lay people. This had significant consequences. The institutionalized regime of the hospital, with its trappings of routines, uniforms and professional hierarchies, became imprinted on the lives of dependent people over the years. Nevertheless, that same medical definition and domination of problems has often saved other groups in the population from a certain form of stigmatization, such stigma stemming in part from Poor Law distinctions between the deserving and undeserving poor. According to those distinctions, those who were able-bodied but not working were labelled as undeserving, but those who were *dependent* (a medically defined definition) and therefore unable to work were designated as deserving. This is the same sort of distinction that has emerged today in attitudes to unemployed people on the one hand, and to chronically sick and disabled people on the other. So, ironically, it has been in one sense advantageous to be medically defined as dependent, but in another it has been disadvantageous because it has meant consignment to certain unacceptable forms of institutionalized care.

More recently, the issue has taken a further twist: as institutionalized care has become stigmatized, so have the medical definitions that go along with it also come under fire. It is a part of the social welfare complex (the personal social services that generally deal with deviant, problem-defined categories, that is, the undeserving) that has sought to take over (and has been given, since the NHS and Community Care Act 1990) the direction of policies relating to the priority groups. They argue that they are best suited to offer care for those who are chronically dependent precisely because they are *not* dominated by the medical model. However, they have overlooked the fact of their own image as being linked to the deviant and the problematic. Thus there is an unfortunate polarization: the medical definition of dependency (acceptable) has tended to ally itself with institutional solutions (unacceptable), and the social welfare definition of dependency (as problematic and therefore unacceptable) has sought to ally itself with the socially acceptable concept of 'community', which turns out to be based on privatized, familial model-type solutions. As a consequence, interprofessional and interagency disputes frequently arise over interpretations as to which of them can offer the best and most appropriate forms of care for chronically and heavily dependent people.

For collective forms of care to be acceptable and non-stigmatizing, it will be necessary to break out of the straitjacket of this interprofessional and interagency competition. The priority groups have certain characteristics in common: they tend to be defined in medical terms but they do not respond to curative treatment; they are dependent because they are in general economically inactive as a result of their condition and therefore have to rely on external support. In these circumstances, dependent people are likely to want to establish clearly that while they may, in limited cases, have medical needs for which medical or other health service treatment may be required, those medical needs should not define their social status. Equally they may also wish to argue that while they need certain forms of welfare support, this does not mean that they are to be seen as problems and labelled as such. Again, it is a question of power and unequal relationships: if health service or social services clients really were clients, they would be able to instruct (in the sense of the archetypal lawyer–client relationship) the providers of welfare as to their needs and requirements. As it is, clients are either suppliants or detainees, dependent on the inclination or otherwise of official service providers. The same is true in the case of the medical definition of dependency – medicalized regimes are imposed on the lives of patients in totality, when all they require is certain defined, and often limited, medical (or nursing) services. The patient has the power of choice removed. Even the contemporary consumer movement, as typified by the Patient's Charter introduced in 1991, with its notion of consumer rights, has done little to alter this.

Alternatives

Criticism is levelled at some current forms of community care provision because, although located in the community, it is said to mimic institutional provision – the size may have been scaled down, but the old medicalized, institutionalized approach remains the same. Any form of residential provision, small units for elderly people and so on, all come in for criticism from this school of argument as if only the family model is acceptable. However, such provision may well offer precisely the size and scope for the collectivist approach to work best. The Scandinavian example of large-scale provision, especially for the elderly, is likely to run the risk of being too large, with a tendency to slip into the impersonalized and alienating styles of the past, although they would argue that there are developed mechanisms for preventing this from happening through concentration on developing smaller subunits within the larger framework. Medium- and small-scale provision, however, offers the convenience of optimum size without having to build in such safeguarding mechanisms, although it may have less to offer in terms of the scale and range of communal facilities.

Within such a setting, the benefits of group living can then be explored. While some of the criticisms of this form of living as being a mere reflection of the institution may be valid, there is no intrinsic reason why that should be so. There are certainly a host of reasons why it might be better than the family model. For example, within a larger group, there is a range of choice in terms of friendship possibilities, leisure activities and household servicing/maintenance functions. Within the narrow confines of the family, on the other hand, there are only limited choices for friendship, biological related-ness very often being the single rationale for its members staying together. Where that relatedness does not exist, as in contrived family model-type arrangements, and where the personal relation-ships do not work well, there is little justification for remaining together, yet service providers *expect* continuity and stability. In a larger setting, there is room for multiple relationships – there is no reason why all members should be *either* dependent people *or* staff.

A number of other people (neither disabled nor staff) could live as part of the group too if it were so decided. A parent might choose to live in such a group setting with a child who had some severe impair-ment, rather than having to choose between living in lonely isolation with the child with all the pressures that that would involve, or parting from the child so that she or he could go into old-style residential care. A mixed group such as this would be far less likely to arouse the suspicion and hostility of people living in the surrounding neighbourhood than is often the case when current community-based provision is proposed; the possibility of integration and acceptance, if residents so chose, would be real. There is no doubt that such communities are feasible and indeed do exist. There is no reason why imaginative service providers, especially with the encour-agement of and experience from the voluntary sector, could not think along these lines. However, organizational and professional rivalry, along with its attached culture and ideologies, needs challenging before that is likely to happen.

At the same time, it is essential that conditions of work within such collective establishments are of an acceptable standard and that there are good standards of pay. The vicious circle of low pay and women's segregation in employment might perhaps then be broken. There is little doubt that women, at present, absorb the cost of caring: they provide free labour power in the home and cheap labour power in the public sphere. Some sources have estimated the hidden costs of informal care at a total of £33.9 billion per annum, compared with £10.1 billion for institutional and professional care combined (Nuttall *et al.*, 1993). Thus society as a whole is simply unaware of the true costs of caring. Whatever model of care is favoured, if it were fully costed, even at low current wage rates, the total cost would be extremely high. Thus the cost of paying the equivalent of a wage to all women caring at home under the family model of care, or the cost of paying a large caring workforce in the public sphere under a collectivist model, would involve a major decision by government on society's behalf to shift resources from other sectors to accommodate such a commitment. Sceptics would say that no government in the near future is likely to make such a decision and would argue that the determinism of economic forces would prevent such choices even being considered. However, there is evidence to suggest the contrary, although from sources further afield. Denmark, for example, spends a far higher proportion of its gross national product on the support of its older population than does the UK (McGlone and Cronin, 1994). From a quite contrary perspective, governments have always been willing to fund sudden wars out of contingency reserves (*pace* Mrs Thatcher's Falklands War and the West's Gulf War). It is ironic that when the 'emergency' relates to the welfare of certain disadvantaged sections of their own population, governments seem to be less willing. The current debate about the unsustainability of state pensions or state support for long-term care is an example of this same paradox. It does not mean, however, that major choices cannot be made in favour of the poor and the dependent.

In spite of the sceptics' opposition, feminists argue that recognition of the true cost of caring must be given and call for a major shift in resource allocation to take account of this. As Thomson (1991) says, it is a question of society's making moral choices about what proportion of its collective resources it wishes to make available for those members of society who are dependent and in need of support. This choice having been made, the case for collective care is then sound – and feasible. The benefits of it are threefold. First, collectivist approaches to living are, in themselves, beneficial to those who adopt them: better social interaction, shared care, greater opportunities for living fuller lives because of better facilities and more resources and so on. Second, the burden of care imposed on women in families regardless of the cost to them in emotional, career and financial terms is alleviated; women should be able to choose what part to play in the fulfilling of society's caring role. Third, those who do choose to care are integrated into the public sphere, receiving appropriate levels of pay to match the socially valued work that they do.

The case is therefore sound in terms of the benefits it would confer on the parties most interested in the issues – women and the dependent people for whom they care. How far, though, are there any indications that its implementation might be feasible? There is no doubt that there is a sharp polarization in the policy options that are presently debated in political and academic discourse and that undoubtedly represent competing ideological value sets. On the right is an emphasis on, on the one hand, privatized solutions to welfare based on a capacity to pay – as seen in the building of private hospitals, clinics, nursing and residential care homes – and, on the other, the fostering of sturdy self-reliance and informal (unpaid) care. On the left is a developing emphasis on the need to take collective responsibility for welfare, but located in and account-able to the 'real needs' of people, as opposed to being fixed in the straitjacket of the old bureaucratic, statist definitions of collec-tivism. The present policy and practice infatuation with community care sits unfortunately and uncomfortably in the middle of this ideological divide, borrowing validation from either side according to circumstance.

Indeed, some of the 'communitarian' thinking coming out of the USA (Etzioni, 1995a, b) and now echoed by the new Labour Party in Britain appears to be uncomfortably individualist in its concep-tion, going against the traditional espousal by the left and centre left of the principle of collective support for the weakest and the most disadvantaged in society. Acceptance of the concept of the underclass, coupled with fear of the uncontained expression of its alienation and dispossession, leads communitarian thinkers to argue for 'sticking plaster' crisis management. Keep rioting youth under control by putting them under curfew, argue the American polemi-cists; promote the advantages of a segmented and discriminating educational system, suggest the new British 'democratic socialists'; blame a generation of parents, especially single parents, already penalized by the harmful consequences of being on the downside of Thatcher's boomtime flowering of individualism – and the new communitarians think they have made the diagnosis and found the solution. The symptoms of the crisis may have been identified correctly – poor parenting, ineffective education, a failure to care – but the causes have been wilfully ignored.

Champions of the right blame the breakdown on the gross expectations created by beliefs in a false notion of community:

> The idea of 'community' is either a meaningless metaphysical abstraction, a banal shorthand description of existing social realities, or a euphemism for State power. No coherent policy proposals can be derived from it. Its only appeal lies in electoral usefulness... it is nostalgic, atavistic, backward-looking, irrational rather than rational. 'Community' is a safe and mythical place, where people can be free of redundancy notices, public expenditure cuts, failed examinations, vandalised telephone booths, teachers on strike, ram raiders, burglaries, cheap imports, VAT on domestic fuel and all the other travails and tribulations of life in modern urban civilisation. (Duncan and Hobson, 1995, p. 11)

However, while their criticism of the lily-livered misconceptions of those supporting the 'community' version of the manifestation of the current crisis is powerfully to the point, the solution that they offer – yet more reliance on the virtues of the free market and its associated individualistic, self-preoccupied solutions – is inadequate. Will Hutton (1995, p. 223) describes critically and persuasively the crisis in contemporary society where 'it is vital to be part of the virtuous upward spirals unleashed by market processes – and not the vicious downward ones' as a result of the pipe-dreams of the new right.

In 1995 the anniversary of the founding of the modern welfare state was celebrated. For the first time in more than a decade, positive things began to be voiced about the benefits conferred on postwar society by the policies of the then new Labour Government. While the case may be overstated if we take the long view and look back to what the historians are beginning to say about support structures in past times, it is true to say that it has been fifty years since it was politically acceptable to talk positively about the virtues of collectivist strategies, about the importance of the strong supporting the weak and about society's duty to take responsibility for all its citizens.

However, I would argue that what I see as the feminist view of collectivism might fit very appropriately into this reappraisal of the past benefits of collectivist strategies. It should thus be feminism's project to develop this and develop a cogent and coherent analysis of the policy implications of a new approach to collectivism. This may, however, be hard. Ten years ago, a volume of the journal *Critical Social Policy* (1986), devoted to feminist issues, made a pertinent point about the lack of success that there had been in integrating feminist analyses into mainstream thinking on the left. It noted that in most social policy analyses from the left, very few of the key texts ever seriously considered the feminist position. It is essential that the feminist view be incorporated and integrated; otherwise it will continue to be marginalized, dealing only with topics and issues deemed to be of women's concern (of which caring is a particular example). Feminist concern with women's issues tends to have the sad consequence of maintaining those issues as the province of women; and men, and the mainstream analysis that they dominate, are happy to consign them to the woman's realm, because it means that they do not have to look at what the implications of the feminist critique really are.

It may be that by seizing on the collectivist trends in thinking that are developing at present, it will be possible to demonstrate the need and efficacy of integrating feminist and mainstream concerns. This would, in turn, mean a strengthening of the opposition to the rightist, residualist view of welfare, which in the last decade has dominated the polar relationship between the two approaches. It is part of the view put forward here that such opposition is likely to succeed and that its case is feasible. Historical evidence shows that the idea of collective involvement in the support of weaker (however defined) sections of the population has persisted through time, even in a society that has traditionally been characterized by a highly developed philosophy of possessive individualism. Indeed there has been a recognition that where the private domain is 'highly private', or highly individualized, the need has often been greatest for collective support for those areas and population categories excluded from it. What the left must seek to do is to demonstrate that collectivism is not only necessary but a good in itself. It must also demonstrate that the collectivist ideal can best be developed and secured by building on those tendencies already existing within present-day

society and integrating with them, rather than by seeking to hive off
collectivist attempts from mainstream society – the history of such
attempts has been fraught with failure.

Nevertheless, it may be difficult to ensure that feminist principles
are incorporated. It is all too easy for the left to pay lip service to the
contribution that it agrees feminism has made to the rethinking of
old dogmas, but it is more difficult for the left to integrate that
thinking into future policy. George and Wilding (1985), for
example, recognize that there was now an acceptance on the left that
the traditional socialist aim of 'reducing inequality' had to be
qualified; it ought to mean, specifically, an aim to reduce inequalities
based on class, gender and race. They agree that it had taken the rise of
the feminist movement (and ironically the growth of the new right)
to 'highlight the importance of the so-called informal sector of
welfare': the family, the wider kin network, neighbours, friends and
voluntary agencies. So far, so good; feminists would hardly disagree.
They have demonstrated the cost that such dependence on the
informal care has for women, while the new right has argued that
such dependence is both necessary and right. George and Wilding
(1985, pp. 144–5) then go on to comment:

> A democratic socialist policy must accept the fact that the contribution
> of the informal sector is vital to the quality of life of many dependent
> people, that they prefer family care, and that families basically want to
> provide such care. Such a policy must, however, also take account of
> what that policy may mean to women and the quality of their lives. For
> the New Right, the mixed economy of welfare is a euphemism for cuts
> in public provision. For the socialist, the term describes a new pattern of
> partnership between statutory and voluntary, formal and informal,
> family and state welfare... A genuine partnership between statutory,
> non-statutory and family norms of social care is the most effective
> method of providing adequate services.

They qualify this by further arguing that the state must provide
adequate funds so that 'the primary burden' does not 'continue to fall
on women as unpaid labour' (although they do not specify how this
might be accomplished). However, nowhere do they acknowledge
that such a strategy would in no real way alter the balance of caring
as it exists at present or in any way alleviate the obligation of caring,
which would still fall on women. They may be paid to do it, but it

would still be a family responsibility, and they would have little freedom to choose whether or not they did it.

Thus there has been a failure to acknowledge that there has to be a much more fundamental change in attitudes towards caring; this has to involve questioning of *male* attitudes to the issue. Why should it continue to be women who are expected to care, either paid or unpaid? And why should it be the familial model of care that is always advocated? It takes a degree of daring to question both these fundamental premises at the same time. When feminists seek to share the burden of caring equally between men and women, by arguing that it should be a non-gendered activity, they appear to be motivated by self-interest; it goes in the face of the culturally conditioned and encouraged altruism that women are always expected to display (Land and Rose, 1985). When they argue specifically against the familial model of care, they appear to be arguing in their interests *against* those who are in need of care. Because of entrenched and deeply held views based on familist ideology, many people find it difficult even to contemplate alternatives to today's accepted wisdom. They also see that accepted wisdom as a fundamentally moral position, so that those who do dare to question it are seen as transgressing the boundaries of acceptable thinking.

These are, however, misconceptions. The feminist alternative is of a society that willingly takes a collective responsibility for all its members, that values the activity of caring and recognizes the worth both of those cared for and those doing the caring. It sees collective responsibility as essentially non-gendered, entering every level and each domain. 'Unpaid', 'voluntary' or 'informal' care is not given a higher moral value than is care provided by the collectivity – such care is too often the outcome of *compulsory* altruism and is exploitative of both giver and receiver. Collective responsibility and collective forms go hand in hand; choice and freedom of action are ensured. Society makes a positive moral choice about resourcing this collectivist approach to caring.

What chance does the feminist case have of succeeding? After the defeat of the left in Britain in four elections, there have been many attempts to regroup and rethink future strategies. There has been an increasing emphasis on democratization and participation (George and Wilding, 1985); the views of women, disabled people, ethnic groups and other minority groups have been acknowledged, and some attempt (however flawed) has been made to incorporate them into mainstream leftist thinking. The traditional vision of socialist society, dominated by centralized and bureaucratized planning and institutions, has finally been rejected. New forms of collectivist organization are being encouraged; greater care is being taken to identify needs as people themselves perceive them, instead of imposing solutions, whether needed or not. The views that feminists can offer about the issue of caring and the wider sphere of welfare should be positively welcomed, although the dominant male view of these same issues will have to be contested.

Times are changing, too, in the existing policy and planning structures presently responsible for the provision of welfare. After a decade of devastating reorganizations and cutbacks, questions are beginning to be raised about the efficacy of recent policies, including community care policies. There is a willingness to look for innovative solutions to the problems of caring (although it would be wrong to suggest that any of these innovations has so far incorporated anything like feminist views). Demands continue to build, however, for a greater resourcing of care for the priority groups, particularly as current policies are perceived to have failed These should be accompanied by demands for changes in current forms of caring.

It is imperative that the left seizes on these 'changing times' and that feminists make certain that their case is incorporated into programmes that are offered as alternatives. Theories of change in social policy emphasize the need to secure legitimacy and support in the process of achieving change; it seems that the further an issue is from the seat of decision making, the more difficult it is to secure that legitimacy or that support (Hall *et al.*, 1978), however feasible, in theory, the application and implementation of the solution might be. It will require the opportunistic seizing of initiative as and when occasions arise for radically new collectivist – and, most importantly – feminist policies to become accepted. This then is the task ahead.

Bibliography

Abbeyfield Society (1989) *The Guide to Abbeyfield Extra Care: the Philosophy of Designing and Caring for the Frail Elderly*, Abbeyfield Society, Potters Bar.

Abel-Smith, B. (1964) *The Hospitals 1800–1948; A Study in Social Administration in England and Wales*, Heinemann, London.

Abrams, P. (1977) Community care: some research problems and priorities, *Policy and Politics*, **6**.

Abrams, P. and McCulloch, A. (1976) *Communes, Sociology and Society*, Cambridge University Press, Cambridge.

Abrams, P. *et al.* (1986) *Creating Care in the Neighbourhood*, ADVANCE, Neighbourhood Care Action Programme, London.

Allen, I. and Perkins, E. (eds) (1995) *The Future of Family Care for Older People*, HMSO, London.

Arber, S. and Ginn, J. (1995) Gender differences in informal caring, *Health and Social Care in the Community*, **3**, 1.

Arber, S., Gilbert, N. and Evandrou, M. (1988) Gender, household composition and receipt of domiciliary services by elderly disabled people, *Journal of Social Policy*, **17**, 2.

Archer, J. and Gruenberg, E. M. (1982) The chronically mentally disabled and 'deinstitutionalization', *Annual Review of Public Health*, **3**.

Arendt, H. (1959) *The Human Condition*, Anchor Books, Garden City.

Audit Commission (1986) *Making a Reality of Community Care*, HMSO, London.

Ayer, S. and Alaszewski, A. (1984) *Community Care and the Mentally Handicapped; Services for Mothers and their Mentally Handicapped Children*, Croom Helm, London.

Baars, J. and Thomese, F. (1994) Communes of elderly people – between independence and colonization, *Journal of Aging Studies*, **8**, 4.

Baker, J. (1979) Social conscience and social policy, *Journal of Social Policy*, **8**, 2.

Baldwin, S. (1995) Love and money: the financial consequences of caring for an older relative. In Allen, I. and Perkins, E. (eds) *The Future of Family Care for Older People*, HMSO, London.

Baldwin, S. and Twigg, J. (1991) Women and community care: reflections on a debate. In Maclean, M. and Groves, D. (eds) *Women's Issues in Social Policy*, Routledge, London.

Barr, D. F. (1977) Residents' evaluation of Hawthorne at Leesburg. Unpublished survey prepared for Marketing Research Department, Colonial Penn Insurance, Philadelphia.

Barrett, M. (1980) *Women's Oppression Today*, Verso, London.

Barrett, M. and McIntosh, M. (1982) *The Anti-social Family*, Verso, London.

Bayley, M. (1973) *Mental Handicap and Community Care*, Routledge & Kegan Paul, London.

Beattie, J. (1964) *Other Cultures*, Routledge & Kegan Paul, London.

Beauvoir, S. de (1972) *The Second Sex*, Penguin, Harmondsworth.

Berger, B. and Berger, P. (1983) *The War Over the Family: Capturing the Middle Ground*, Penguin, Harmondsworth.

Bernard, J. (1971) *Women and the Public Interest*, Aldine/Atherton, Chicago.

Berthoud, R. (1991) Meeting the costs of disability. In Dalley, G. (ed.) *Disability and Social Policy*, Policy Studies Institute, London.

Bertolt, A. and Bertolt, P. (1983) Comprehensive centres for the elderly in Denmark, *Update*, **27**, 7.

Blaxter, M. (1976) *The Meaning of Disability*, Heinemann, London.

Bohannon, P. (1954) *Tiv Farm and Settlement*, HMSO, London.

Booth, T. (1985) *Home Truths: Old People's Homes and the Outcome of Care*, Gower, Aldershot.

Bowlby, J. (1953) *Child Care and the Growth of Love*, Penguin, Harmondsworth.

Bowlby, J. (1984) *Attachment and Loss, Vol 1: Attachment*, Penguin, Harmondsworth.

Brisenden, S. (1989) A charter for personal care, *Disablement Income Group Progress*, **16**.

Brody, E. (1981) Women in the middle and family help to other people, *The Gerontologist*, **21**.

Brown, C. and Thompson, K. (1994) A quality life: searching for quality of life in residential services for elderly people, *Australian Journal on Ageing*, **13**, 3.

Brown, G. and Harris, T. (1978) *The Social Origins of Depression*, Tavistock, London.

Brown, G. and Wright, T. (eds) (1995) *Values, Visions and Voices: An Anthology of Socialism*, Mainstream Publishing, Edinburgh.

Brown, H. and Smith, H. (eds) (1992) *Normalisation: A Reader for the Nineties*, Tavistock/Routledge, London.

Bruegel, I. (1978) What keeps the family going? *International Socialism*, **2**, 1.

Buch, P. (1973) Introduction. In Rodinson, M. *Israel, A Colonial Settler State?* Monad Press/Pathfinder Press, New York.

Bujra, J. (1978) Introductory: female solidarity and the sexual division of labour. In Caplan, P. and Bujra, J. *Women United, Women Divided: Cross-cultural Perspectives on Female Solidarity*, Tavistock, London.

Bulmer, M. (1987) *The Social Basis of Community Care*, Allen and Unwin, London.

Butler, A., Oldman, C. and Greve, C. (1983) *Sheltered Housing for the Elderly: Policy, Practice and the Consumer*, George Allen & Unwin, London.

Callan, H. and Ardener, S. (1984) *The Incorporated Wife*, Croom Helm, London.

Caplan, P. and Bujra, J. (eds) (1978) *Women United, Women Divided: Cross-cultural Perspectives on Female Solidarity*, Tavistock, London.

Central Statistical Office (1995) *Social Trends: 1995 Edition*, HMSO, London.

Clay, R. M. (1909) *The Mediaeval Hospitals of England*, Methuen, London.

Cohen, G. (1978) Women's solidarity and the preservation of privilege. In Caplan, P. and Bujra, J. (eds) *Women United, Women Divided: Cross-cultural Perspectives on Female Solidarity*, Tavistock, London.

Collins, J. (1995) Living difficulties, *Community Care*, 25 May.

Comer, L. (1973) Functions of the family under capitalism. Unpublished paper.

Community Care (1984) Children in care, *Community Care*, 5 January.

Cooper, D. (1971) *The Death of the Family*, Penguin, Harmondsworth.

Coote, A. (1985) Labour: the feminist touch, *Marxism Today*, **29**, 11.

Cox, C. and Pearson, M. (1995) *Made To Care: the Case for Residential and Village Communities for People with a Mental Handicap*, The Rannoch Trust, London.

Critical Social Policy, (1986) **16**.

Cunnison, S. and Page, D. (1984) *For the Rest of Their Days? A Study of the Council's Sheltered Housing Schemes in Hull*, Humberside College of Higher Education, Hull.

Dalley, G. (1983) Ideologies of care: a feminist contribution to the debate, *Critical Social Policy*, **8**.

Dalley, G. (1989) Community care: the ideal and the reality. In Brechin, A. and Walmsley, J. (eds) *Making Connections: Reflecting on the Lives and Experiences of People with Learning Difficulties*, Hodder & Stoughton/ Open University, London.

Dalley, G. (ed.) (1991) *Disability and Social Policy*, Policy Studies Institute, London.

Dalley, G. (1992) Social welfare ideologies and normalisation: links and conflicts. In Brown, H. and Smith, H (eds) *Normalisation: A Reader for the Nineties*, Tavistock/Routledge, London.

Dalley, G. (1993) Caring: a legitimate interest of older women. In Bernard, M. and Meade, K. (eds) *Women Come of Age: Perspectives on the Lives of Older Women*, Edward Arnold, London.

Davis, A. and Brook, E. (1985) Women and social work. In Brook, E. and

168   *Ideologies of Caring*

Davis, A. (eds) *Women, the Family and Social Work*, Tavistock, London.
Dearman, E. G. (1982) Sun City: care for the elderly in Arizona, *Social Policy and Administration*, **16**, 3.
Dennis, N. and Erdos, G. (1992) *Families without Fathers*, Institute of Economic Affairs, London.
Department of Health (1989a) *Caring for People: Community Care in the Next Decade and Beyond*, HMSO, London.
Department of Health (1989b) *Working for Patients*, HMSO, London.
Department of Health (1994) *Health and Personal Social Services Statistics for England*, HMSO, London.
Department of Health (1995) *NHS Responsibilities for Meeting Continuing Health Care Needs*, NHS Executive, Department of Health, Leeds.
DHSS (Department of Health and Social Security) (1971a) *Better Services for the Mentally Handicapped*, Cmnd. 4683, HMSO, London.
DHSS (Department of Health and Social Security) (1971b) *Report of Committee of Inquiry into Allegations of Ill-treatment of Patients and Other Irregularities at the Ely Hospital Cardiff*, Cmnd. 3795, HMSO, London.
DHSS (Department of Health and Social Security) (1975) *Better Services for the Mentally Ill*, Cmnd. 6233, HMSO, London.
DHSS (Department of Health and Social Security) (1976) *Priorities for Health and Personal Social Services in England: A Consultative Document*, HMSO, London.
DHSS (Department of Health and Social Security) (1977) *The Way Forward*, HMSO, London.
DHSS (Department of Health and Social Security) (1981a) *Care in Action: A Handbook of Policies and Priorities for the Health and Personal Social Services in England*, HMSO, London.
DHSS (Department of Health and Social Security) (1981b) *Growing Older*, Cmnd. 8173, HMSO, London.
Dobash, R. E. and Dobash, R. (1980) *Violence Against Wives: A Case Against Patriarchy*, Open Books, London.
Donald, S. and Gordon, D. S. (1991) *Informal Care and Older People – Survey Results from the Aberdeen Informal Support and Care Project*, Age Concern Scotland, Edinburgh.
Duncan, A. and Hobson, D. (1995) *Saturn's Children: How the State Devours Liberty, Prosperity, and Virtue*, Sinclair-Stevenson, London.
Dunleavy, P. (1981) Professions and policy change: notes towards a model of ideological corporatism, *Public Administration Bulletin*, **36**.
Dunning, A. (1995) *Citizen Advocacy with Older People: A Code of Good Practice*, Centre for Policy on Ageing, London.
Durkheim, E. (1960) *The Division of Labour in Society*, Free Press, New York.
Ensomme Gamles Vaern (1980) Housing desires of the elderly – review, *Ageing International*, **7**, 2.
Equal Opportunities Commission (1982) *Caring for the Elderly and Handicapped: Community Care Policies and Women's Lives*, EOC, Manchester.

Etzioni, A. (1995a) Common values, *New Statesman and Society*, 12 May.

Etzioni, A. (1995b) *Spirit of Community: Rights, Responsibilities and Communitarianism*, Fontana Books, London.

Evandrou, M. (1990) *Challenging the Invisibility of Carers*, Paper WSP/49, STICERD, London School of Economics, London.

Evers, H. (1981) Care or custody? The experience of women patients in long stay geriatric wards. In Williams, G. and Hutter, B. (eds) *Controlling Women – The Normal and the Deviant*, Croom Helm, London.

Fallers, L. A. (1961) Ideology and culture in Uganda nationalism, *American Anthropologist*, **63**, 19.

Family Policy Studies Centre (1994) *Families in the European Union*, FPSC, London.

Feeley, D. (1972) The family. In Jenness, L. *Feminism and Socialism*, Pathfinder Press, New York.

Finch, J. (1983) *Married to the Job: Wives Incorporation in Men's Work*, George Allen & Unwin, London.

Finch, J. (1984) Community care: developing non-sexist alternatives, *Critical Social Policy*, **9**.

Finch, J. (1995) Responsibilities, obligations and commitments. In Allen, I. and Perkins, E. (eds) *The Future of Family Care for Older People*, HMSO, London.

Finch, J. and Groves, D. (1980) Community care and the family: a case for equal opportunities, *Journal of Social Policy*, **9**, 4.

Finch, J. and Groves, D. (eds) (1983) *A Labour of Love: Women, Work and Caring*, Routledge & Kegan Paul, London.

Finch, J. and Groves, D. (1985) Old girl, old boy: gender divisions in social work with the elderly. In Davis, A. and Brook, E (eds) *Women, the Family and Social Work*, Tavistock, London.

Flandrin, J.-L. (1979) *Families in Former Times: Kinship, Household and Sexuality*, Cambridge University Press, Cambridge.

Fortes, M. (1969) *Kinship and the Social Order: the Legacy of Lewis Henry Morgan*, Aldine, Chicago.

Friedman, M. and Friedman, R. (1980) *Free to Choose*, Penguin, Harmondsworth.

Garner, L. (1984) *Stepping Stones to Women's Liberty: Feminist Ideas in the Women's Suffrage Movement, 1900–18*, Heinemann/Gower, Aldershot.

Gavron, H. (1966) *The Captive Wife*, Penguin, Harmondsworth.

George, V. and Wilding, P. (1985) *Ideology and Social Welfare*, 2nd edn, Routledge & Kegan Paul, London.

Gilhooly, M. (1984) The impact of care giving on care givers, *British Journal of Medical Psychology*, **57**.

Gittins, D. (1985) *The Family in Question: Changing Households and Familiar Ideologies*, Macmillan, London.

Glendinning, C. (1983) *Unshared Care: Parents and their Disabled Children*, Routledge & Kegan Paul, London.

Glendinning, C. (1992) *The Costs of Informal Care: Looking Inside the*

Household, SPRU Discussion Paper, HMSO, London.

Godfrey, W. H. (1955) *The English Almshouse, with Some Account of its Predecessor, the Medieval Hospital,* Faber, London.

Goody, E. N. (1982) *Parenthood and Social Reproduction: Fostering and Occupational Roles in West Africa,* Cambridge University Press, Cambridge.

Graham, H. (1983) Caring: a labour of love. In Finch, J. and Groves, D. (eds) *A Labour of Love: Women, Work and Caring,* Routledge & Kegan Paul, London.

Green, D. (1992) Liberty, poverty and the underclass: a classical–liberal approach to public policy. In Smith, D. (ed.) *Understanding the Underclass,* Policy Studies Institute, London.

Green, H. (1988) Informal Carers, *OPCS Series GHS, No.15, Supplement A,* HMSO, London.

Greer, G. (1971) *The Female Eunuch,* Paladin, London.

Greer, G. (1985) *Sex and Destiny: The Politics of Human Fertility,* Picador, London.

Griffiths, Sir R. (1988) *Community Care: an Agenda for Action: a report to the Secretary of State for Social Services, (the Griffiths Report),* HMSO, London.

Grundy, E. (1995) Demographic influences on the future of family care. In Allen, I. and Perkins, E. (eds) *The Future of Family Care for Older People,* HMSO, London.

Hall, P., Land, H., Parker, R. and Webb, A. (1978) *Change, Choice and Conflict in Social Policy,* Heinemann, London.

Hancock, R. and Jarvis, C. (1994) *The Long Term Effects of Being a Carer,* Age Concern Institute of Gerontology, King's College/HMSO, London.

Hardy, D. (1979) *Alternative Communities in Nineteenth Century England,* Longman, London.

Hardy, J. (1981) *Values in Social Policy: Nine Contradictions,* Routledge & Kegan Paul, London.

Harris, R. (1985) Endpoints and starting points: some critical remarks on Janet Finch's 'Community care: developing non-sexist alternatives', *Critical Social Policy,* **12**.

Hayek, F. A. (1976) *Law, Legislation and Liberty, Vol. 2, The Mirage of Social Justice,* Routledge & Kegan Paul, London.

Hicks, C. (1988) *Who Cares: Looking after People at Home,* Virago, London.

Himmelfarb, G. (1985) *The Idea of Poverty: England in the Early Industrial Age,* Faber, London.

House of Commons (1985) *Community Care with Special Reference to Adult Mentally Ill and Mentally Handicapped People. Second Report from the Social Services Select Committee, Session 1984–85,* HMSO, London.

Hunt, A. (1970) *The Home Help Service in England and Wales,* HMSO, London.

Hutton, W. (1995) *The State We're In,* Jonathan Cape, London.

Illsley, R. (1981) Problems of dependency groups: the care of the elderly, the handicapped and the chronically ill, *Social Science and Medicine*, **15A**.

International Marxist Group (1972) Women, the unions and work... what must be done? A reply by V. Jones to Selma James. Unpublished paper.

International Socialists (1970) *Women's Newsletter*, December.

Irvine, E. (1980) *The Family in the Kibbutz*, Study Commission on the Family, London.

Jansen, E. (1980) *The Therapeutic Community*, Croom Helm, London.

Jones, K. (1972) *A History of the Mental Health Services*, Routledge & Kegan Paul, London.

Jones, K. and Poletti, A. (1985) Understanding the Italian experience, *British Journal of Psychiatry*, **146**.

Joseph, K. (1976) *Stranded on the Middle Ground*, Centre for Policy Studies, London.

Joseph, K. and Sumption, J. (1979) *Equality*, John Murray, London.

Kahn, R. L. and Antonucci, T. (1981) Convoys over the life course: attachment, roles and social support. In Baltes, P. B. and Brim, O. (eds) *Life Span Development and Behavior*, Academic Press, New York.

Kanter, R. M. (1972) *Commitment and Community: Communes and Utopias in Sociological Perspective*, Harvard University Press, Cambridge, Mass.

Keesing, R. M. (1975) *Kin Groups and Social Structure*, Holt Reinhart & Winston, New York.

Kestenbaum, A. (1993) *An Opportunity Lost? Social Services Use of the Independent Living Transfer*, Disablement Income Group, London.

Kollontai, A. (1971) *Communism and the Family*, Pluto Press, London.

Laing, R. D. (1985) What is asylum. In Terrington, R. (ed.) *Towards a Whole Society. Collected papers on Aspects of Mental Health*, Richmond Fellowship Press, London.

Lakey, J. (1994) *Disabled People and the Independent Living Fund*, Policy Studies Institute, London.

Land, H. (1978) Who cares for the family? *Journal of Social Policy*, 7, 3.

Land, H. and Rose, H. (1985) Compulsory altruism for some or an altruistic society for all? In Bean, P., Ferris, J. and Whynes, D. (eds) *In Defence of Welfare*, Tavistock, London.

Laslett, P. and Wall, R. (eds.) (1972) *Household and Family in Past Times*, Cambridge University Press, Cambridge.

Le Gros Clarke, F. (1948) *Social History of the School Meals Service*, London Council of Social Services/National Council of Social Service, London.

Leach, P. (1979) *Who Cares?* Penguin, Harmondsworth.

Leff, J. (1993) Evaluating community placement of long-stay psychiatric patients, *British Journal of Psychiatry*, **162**, Supplement 19.

Leval, G. (1975) *Collectives in the Spanish Revolution*, Freedom Press, London.

Levin, E., Sinclair, I. and Gorbach, P. (1985) The effectiveness of the home help service with confused old people and their families, *Research, Policy and Planning*, **3**, 2.

Lewis, J. (1984) *Women in England 1870–1950: Sexual Divisions and Social*

Change, Wheatsheaf, Brighton.

Lewis, J. and Meredith, B. (1988) *Daughters who Care: Daughters Caring for Mothers at Home*, Routledge & Kegan Paul, London.

Llewelyn-Davies, Margaret (1978) *Maternity: Letters from Working Women*, Virago, London.

Llewelyn-Davies, Melissa (1978) Two contexts of solidarity. In Caplan, P. and Bujra, J. (eds) *Women United, Women Divided: Cross-cultural Perspectives on Female Solidarity*, Tavistock, London.

Lukes, S. (1973) *Individualism*, Basil Blackwell, Oxford.

Macfarlane, A. (1978) *The Origins of English Individualism*, Basil Blackwell, Oxford.

McGlone, F. and Cronin, N. (1994) *A Crisis in Care? The Future of Family and State Care for Older People in the European Union*, FPSC/CPA, London.

Macpherson, C. B. (1962) *The Political Theory of Possessive Individualism*, Oxford University Press, Oxford.

Maher, V. (1976) Kin, clients and accomplices: relations among women in Morocco. In Barker, D. and Allen, S. (eds) *Sexual Divisions and Society: Process and Change*, Tavistock, London.

Manning, N. and Oliver, M. (1985) Madness, epilepsy and medicine. In Manning, N. (ed.) *Social Problems and Welfare Ideology*, Gower, Aldershot.

Marx, K. and Engels, F. (1973) *Selected Works*, Lawrence & Wishart, London.

Marx, K. and Engels, F. (1974) *The German Ideology* (ed. C. J. Arthur), Lawrence & Wishart, London.

Meacher, M. (1982) *Socialism with a Human Face*, George Allen & Unwin, London.

Means, R. and Smith, R. (1983) From public assistance institutions to 'Sunshine Hotels': changing state perceptions about residential care for the elderly. In Jerrome, D. (ed.) *Ageing in Modern Society*, Croom Helm, London.

Ministry of Health (1962) *A Hospital Plan for England and Wales*, Cmnd. 1604, HMSO, London.

Mitchell, J. (1966) Women: the longest revolution, *New Left Review*, **40**.

Morris, J. (1991) *Pride against Prejudice*, The Women's Press, London.

Morris, J. (1993) *Independent Lives: Community Care and Disabled People*, Macmillan, London.

Mount, F. (1981) *The Subversive Family*, Cape, London.

Murray, C. (1984) *Losing Ground: American Social Policy, 1950–1980*, Basic Books, New York.

Murray, C. (1990) *The Emerging British Underclass*, IEA, London.

NCVO (1995) More care cash needed, *NCVO News*, June.

Nelson, N. (1978) Women must help each other. In Caplan P. and Bujra, J. (eds) *Women United, Women Divided: Cross-cultural Perspectives on Female Solidarity*, Tavistock, London.

New, C. and David, M. (1985) *For the Children's Sake*, Penguin, Harmondsworth.

Nisbet, R. (1974) *The Social Philosophers*, Heinemann, London.

Nottingham Women's Liberation Theory Group (1974) Marked 'Private'. In *Women and Socialism Conference Paper 3*, Birmingham.

Nuttall, S.R. *et al.* (1993) *Financing Long-term Care in Great Britain*, Institute of Actuaries, London.

Oakley, A. (1974) *The Sociology of Housework*, Martin Robertson, Oxford.

Oliver, M. (1991) Speaking out: disabled people and state welfare. In Dalley, G. (ed.) *Disability and Social Policy*, Policy Studies Institute, London.

OPCS (Office of Population Censuses and Surveys) (1993) *General Household Survey*, Series GHS No. 24, HMSO, London.

Pahl, J. (1980) Patterns of money management, *Journal of Social Policy*, **9**, 3.

Parker, G. and Lawton, D. (1994) *Different Types of Care, Different Types of Carer: Evidence from the General Household Survey*, SPRU, HMSO, London.

Parker, R. (1981) Tending and social policy. In Goldberg, E. M. and Hatch, S. (eds) *A New Look at the Personal Social Services*, Discussion Paper 4, Policy Studies Institute, London.

Peace, S. M. (1984) *Shared Living: A Viable Alternative for the Elderly?* International Federation on Ageing, Washington.

Pearson, R. (1982) Scandinavia keeps them active, *New Age*, **18**.

Pelling, M. and Smith, R. M. (eds) (1991) *Life, Death and the Elderly: Historical Perspectives*, Routledge, London.

Peristiany, J. G. (ed.) (1974) *Honour and Shame: The Values of Mediterranean Society*, University of Chicago Press, Chicago.

Pinker, R. (1979) *Social Theory and Social Policy*, Heinemann Educational Books, London.

Pitt-Rivers, J. (1973) The kith and the kin. In Goody, J. (ed.) *The Character of Kinship*, Cambridge University Press, Cambridge.

Pollock, L. (1983) *Forgotten Children: Parent–Child Relations from 1500 to 1900*, Cambridge University Press, Cambridge.

Radcliffe-Brown, A. R. (1964) *The Andaman Islanders*, Free Press of Glencoe, New York.

Richards, V. (1975) Foreword. In Leval, G. (1975) *Collectives in the Spanish Revolution*, Freedom Press, London.

Rigby, A. (1974) *Alternative Realities: A Study of Communes and Their Members*, Routledge & Kegan Paul, London.

Rimmer, L. (1981) *Families in Focus: Marriage, Divorce and Family Patterns*, Study Commission on the Family, London.

Rodinson, M. (1973) *Israel: A Colonial Settler State?* Monad Press/ Pathfinder Press, New York.

Rogers, B. (1980) *The Domestication of Women: Discrimination in Developing Societies*, Tavistock, London.

Rowbotham, S. (1972) Women's liberation and the new politics. In

174   *Ideologies of Caring*

Wandor, M. (ed.) *The Body Politic,* Stage 1, London.
Rowbotham, S. (1973) *Hidden from History,* Pluto Press, London.
Rowlingson, K. and Berthoud, R. (1994) *Evaluating the Disability Working Allowance,* Policy Studies Institute, London.
Russell, D. (1983) *The Dora Russell Reader: 57 Years of Writing and Journalism 1925–1982,* Pandora Press, London.
Saladin d'Anglure, B. (1967) *L'Organisation Sociale Traditionelle des Esquimaux de Kangirsujuaaq (Nouveau Quebec),* Centre d'Etudes Nordiques, Leval University, Canada.
Secombe, W. (1974) The housewife and her labour, *New Left Review,* **83**.
Sharma, U. (1978) Segregation and its consequences. In Caplan, P. and Bujra, J. (eds) *Women United, Women Divided: Cross-cultural Perspectives on Female Solidarity,* Tavistock, London.
Shearer, A. (1982a) *Living Independently,* Centre on Environment for the Handicapped/King Edward's Hospital Fund for London, London.
Shearer, A. (1982b) *An Ordinary Life: Issues and Strategies for Training Staff for Community Mental Handicap Services,* King's Fund Project Paper No. 42, King's Fund Centre, London.
Smith, J. E. (1984) Widowhood and ageing in traditional English society, *Ageing and Society,* **4**, 4.
Smith, M. G. (1960) *Government in Zazzau, 1800–1950,* Oxford University Press, London.
Smith, R. M. (1984) The structured dependence of the elderly as a recent development: some sceptical historical thoughts, *Ageing and Society,* **4**, 4.
Solanas, V. (1971) *Society for Cutting Up Men (SCUM) Manifesto,* Olympia Press, London.
Spencer, P. (1965) *The Samburu: A Study of Gerontocracy in a Nomadic Tribe,* Routledge & Kegan Paul, London.
Spiro, M. (1954) Is the family universal? *American Anthropologist,* **56**, 5.
Stedman Jones, G. (1985) Paternalism revisited, *Marxism Today,* **29**, 7.
Streib, G. F., Folts, E. and Hilker, M. A. (1984) *Old Homes – New Families: Shared Housing for the Elderly,* Columbia University Press, New York.
Tawney, R. H. (1964) *The Radical Tradition,* Penguin, Harmondsworth.
Tebbit, N. (1986) Speech at St James's, Piccadilly, Conservative Central Office, London.
Thomas, C. (1993) Community care: the reality, *International Journal of Geriatric Psychiatry,* **8**, 12.
Thompson, J. D. and Goldin, G. (1975) *The Hospital: A Social and Architectural History,* Yale University Press, New Haven.
Thomson, D. (1983) The decline of social welfare: falling state support for the elderly since early Victorian times, *Ageing and Society,* **3**, 1.
Thomson, D. (1991) The welfare of the elderly in the past: a family or community responsibility? In Pelling, M. and Smith, R. M. (eds) *Life, Death and the Elderly: Historical Perspectives,* Routledge, London.
Titmuss, R. (1979) Community care: fact or fiction. In Titmuss, R. (ed.) *Commitment to Welfare,* George Allen & Unwin, London.

Tonnies, F. (1955) *Gemeinschaft and Gesellschaft* (*Community and Association*, (trans. C. S. Loomis), Routledge & Kegan Paul, London.

Torres, S. and Trotzky, E. (1982) 'Life-care' communities: independence, security for older Americans, *Hospital Progress*, **63**, 2.

Townsend, P. (1962) *The Last Refuge: A Survey of Residential Institutions and Homes for the Aged in England and Wales*, Routledge & Kegan Paul, London.

Twigg, J. (ed.) (1992) *Carers: Research and Practice*, HMSO, London.

Ungerson, C. (1983) Women and caring: skills, tasks and taboos. In Gamarnikov, E. *et al.* (eds) *The Public and the Private*, Heinemann, London.

Ungerson, C. (1987) *Policy is Personal: Sex, Gender and Informal Caring*, Tavistock, London.

Vladeck, B. (1980) *Unloving Care: The Nursing Home Tragedy*, Basic Books, New York.

Wandor, M. (ed.) (1972) *The Body Politic: Writings from the Women's Liberation Movement in Britain 1969–1972*, Stage 1, London.

Weale, A. (1990) Does the community mind enough? *Nursing Times*, **86**, 27.

Wear, A. (1986) Illness in strange places. Unpublished paper presented to Wellcome History of Medicine seminar, London, 29 January.

White, K. (1986) A shared life, *Community Care*, 30 January.

Whitehouse, A. (1984) Just what the doctor ordered, *Community Care*, 20 December.

Wilkin, D. (1979) *Caring for the Mentally Handicapped Child*, Croom Helm, London.

Willetts, D. (1992) *Modern Conservatism*, Penguin, Harmondsworth.

Williams, G. H. (1983) The movement for independent living: an evaluation and critique, *Social Science and Medicine*, **17**, 15.

Wing, L. (1990) Closing Darenth Park Mental Handicap Hospital: the effects on residents. In Segal, S. (ed.) *The Place of Villages and Residential Communities*, AB Academic, Bicester, Oxon.

Wolfensberger, W. (1972) *The Principle of Normalization in Human Services*, National Institute on Mental Retardation, Downsview, Toronto.

Wolfensberger, W. (1983) Social role valorization: a new term for the principle of normalization, *Mental Retardation*, **21**, 6.

Wood, R. (1991) Care of disabled people. In Dalley, G. (ed.) *Disability and Social Policy*, Policy Studies Institute, London.

Woodward, J. (1974) *To Do the Sick No Harm: A Study of the British Voluntary Hospital System to 1875*, Routledge & Kegan Paul, London.

Wright, F. (1986) *Left to Care Alone*, Gower, Aldershot.

Young, P. (1985) Denmark: a utopia for the old, *New Age*, **29**.

Name index ·

Subject Index

A

aged people *see* older people

almshouses, 110, 116, 117

altruism, 18, 21, 23–5, 48, 50, 51, 54, 108, 120, 128, 148, 149
  compulsory, 23–4, 163
  prescribed, 71

American Perfectionists, 79

anarchism, 51–2, 54, 81–2, 89
  communist, 82
  religious, 82

Andaman Islanders, 103

asylum, need for, 10, 24, 143

attachment, mother–child, 29, 101–2

B

Bethlem, Bedlam, 117

Blue Spring community, 80

C

Camphill villages, 143

capitalism, 38, 39, 40, 42, 43, 45–6, 90, 119, 120

care, burden of, 11, 12, 13, 106, 108, 109, 121, 130
  collectivist principles of, 105, 122–5, 128–33
  costs of, 158
  feminists and, 65–8
  nature of, 13–15
  standards of, Chapter 6 *passim*

Chartist communities, 81

childcare, 29, 31, 54, 58, 59, 60, 61, 62, 64, 65, 67, 88, 101–5, 133–7, 153

children in care, 32–3, 136

chronically sick and dependent people *see* dependent people

Church, the, 105, 109, 116

class, 22, 38–42, 51, 70, 85, 90, 93, 105, 111, 118, 141

Clousden Hill community, 22

collective living schemes, 137–43

collectivism, Chapter 3 *passim*
  definitions of, 49–52
  and feminism, 57–64

communal feeding, 58, 59, 60, 61, 63, 64, 76, 79, 81, 137, 138, 139

communal living, 57, 62, 64, 70, 73, 79–84, 88–9, 131, 140

communes, 72–3, 82, 89, 92–3

communitarianism, 56, 159, 160

community
  meaning of, 54–6, 155
  spirit, 96, 131

community care policies, 5, 6, 7, 8, 9, 10, 11, 12, 24, 25, 54–5, 66, 96, 97, 121, 131, 143, 155, 159

community mental health centres, 8

communities, religious/sectarian, 73, 78–82
  alternative, 73, 82, 93

'convoy' concept, 139

Co-operative and Economical Society, 88

D

daily living, 28–9, Chapter 4 *passim*

de-institutionalization, 5, 31